MW00890083

KEYS TO SUCCESSFUL LEADERSHIP

Developing the mindset and skills
of a great leader

Número de registro: 2401296787398
ISBN: 9798325671050

Dedicated to my father, a great leader.
The person who has inspired me the most
throughout my life.

INDEX

WHY AM I WRITING THIS BOOK?

I remember the first time I had to lead a team. It was a very important change in my professional career, in fact, one of the most difficult challenges I have had to face in my life. At that time I was working in a multinational company where, in recognition of my performance, I was promoted until one day I was leading a team.

I went from flowing with my job as a product engineer in Ireland, to seeming stuck in my new role as Supply Chain Operations Manager in the Netherlands. It was my first experience managing people. I did not know how to lead a team as I had not been taught it at university or in any of my previous positions. Suddenly, I felt the great need to develop my leadership and other skills to cope with my new responsibilities.

I not only experienced this situation firsthand, but it is very common in organizations that request my services for the *Development of Leaders and High Performance Teams.*

*Many managers have been promoted as
a reward and recognition for a job well
done and suddenly, although they are great
professionals, they do not know how to
perform their new position in front of a team.
The good news is that this situation
has a solution.*

In this book I present the skills that I needed to learn back in the day, when I was promoted and had to lead a team for the first time. Interestingly, these skills are the ones my clients ask me for the most, both in individual processes and in my In Company workshops for management and middle management teams.

In my first book, *Motivated Teams, Productive Teams*, I discussed those methodologies and tools that everyone who leads people should know in order to achieve a high performance team.

In this book, however, I focus mainly on the leader himself. Here I want to expose what skills, methodologies and tools everyone leading a team should know in order to achieve greater productivity, motivation and professional and personal growth.

I was very fortunate, once I identified my areas for improvement, to have the training and coaching to perform my new role leading a team. And now I have the great fortune to have as clients companies and leaders who detect these needs and seek help to solve them.

The purpose of this book is to provide these professionals, who suddenly find themselves in a new situation (leading a team, increased responsibilities, new roles...), with a guide to help them achieve better results. A guide for managers facing new challenges.

We will see four blocks:

Self-leadership and mindset for excellence. We will review from the importance of knowing oneself and adopting good habits, to how to manage difficult moments, failure or stress.

The social intelligence of a leader. We will highlight the importance of interacting with others, communicating assertively, taking care of our personal relationships and the impression we leave on others.

The leader's productivity. One of the scarcest resources a leader can have is time, and therefore it is essential that as we take on more responsibilities and when we lead a team, we learn to optimize every minute of our day. We will see how priorities change when we have a team, and some techniques that can help us to be more productive. I develop this topic in more depth in my book *Productivity for Leaders.*

Team leadership. This is probably one of the most complicated tasks anyone can encounter in their professional life. The way we manage our teams can have a tremendous impact on their performance and motivation. Although I develop this topic in more depth in my book *Motivated Teams, Productive Teams*, here we will review the main guidelines to keep in mind when leading people and some additional concepts.

Equipping ourselves with tools and methodologies that help us on a daily basis will improve our performance and that of our teams, and we will even be able to enjoy our jobs.

PART 1:

SELF-LEADERSHIP

AND MINDSET FOR EXCELLENCE

- THE IMPORTANCE OF SELF-KNOWLEDGE
- EMOTIONAL INTELLIGENCE
- THE HABITS OF EXCELLENCE
- STRESS MANAGEMENT AND BURNOUT
- LEARNING FROM MISTAKES
- SHARPEN THE SAW
- NEVER STOP LEARNING

THE IMPORTANCE OF SELF-KNOWLEDGE

It has been proven that the most effective people are those who know themselves, their abilities and weaknesses, so they are able to develop strategies that respond to the demands of their environment.

In order to move forward, it is essential to know ourselves in depth, to know our strengths, our areas of improvement and our motivators.

HOW TO DEVELOP OUR POTENTIAL

Let's take a look at four steps that will help us discover our best version:

Step 1: Take inventory of your personal resources. Until we are aware of what we have, we will not be able to take advantage of it. Nor can we improve anything until we become aware of our limitations. It is about making an inventory of strengths, opportunities, points of improvement and threats where we can evaluate everything that can help us to advance, or on the contrary can hinder or limit our progress.

Tools such as the SWOT would allow us to make this inventory at a personal level, analyzing both internal factors (strengths and weaknesses) and external factors (threats and opportunities).

	Helpful	**Harmful**
Internal Origin	**S** STRENGTHS	**W** WEAKNESSES
External Origin	**O** OPPORTUNITIES	**T** THREATS

Step 2: Identify your motivators. It is very important to know what moves us, what fills us and motivates us, what we are passionate about and that can be our engine in difficult times. That passion can even make the difference between success and failure.

Many times, we may encounter difficulties when performing this type of inventory, especially when it comes to evaluate ourselves, our skills, motivations, etc... Fortunately, there are tools on the market with a scientific basis and with an enormous reliability that can greatly facilitate this task of self-knowledge. For example, some people are highly motivated to lead teams while others may find it uncomfortable and tedious. This can have a great influence when it comes to accepting and exercising a position as a manager.

Step 3: Capitalize on your strengths and opportunities.
Once we have this phase of self-knowledge resolved, we should try to answer these questions: What can we improve? How can I enhance my strengths? How can we take advantage of all this? It is about seeking the maximum benefit from all those strengths and opportunities that are presented to us.

Step 4: Minimize your limitations. We have to work on our areas of improvement and obstacles to minimize their impact on achieving our goals. Are you missing a key competency to achieve your goals? What could you do to acquire it? I want to make an aside on this topic: there are times when a limitation can be worked on in such a way that it is not only overcome, but can become a strength.

An example: At the end of the 19th century, Joseph Pilates was born, a child with rickets, rheumatism and asthma. This child, in spite of all his health problems and physical limitations, had a great strength: his eagerness to excel. At the age of fourteen he was already an athlete and later, Pilates not only overcame his physical limitations, but also developed the Pilates Method. Who could have predicted to this rickety, asthmatic and rheumatic child that he would reach such an advanced age in such excellent physical shape?

LEADER SELF-KNOWLEDGE

The first step in working on our leadership is to know ourselves as leaders. We cannot improve if we do not know where we need to focus.

Most of us think we already know ourselves, and maybe it's

true that we have a good idea of what we look like, but we can't be objective with ourselves.

The Johari window displays the following matrix divided into four areas, defined by the information that is transmitted about us:

	I know	I do not know
The others know	Free area	Blind area
The others do not know	Secret area	Hidden area

According to this, there will be areas of us that others see that we are unable to perceive. Can you imagine what others can see in you that you are not able to see? Would you like to know?

Each and every one of us has strengths and areas for improvement, some of which we already know, but there are others of which we are not aware.

The image we have of ourselves is a biased vision that should be contrasted. The first step to improve is to identify areas for improvement, without this step we will hardly make progress.

When I work with managers on an individual level in *Leadership Development* processes, the first step of all is this exercise of self-knowledge that will be the basis for the rest of the process.

There are many tools on the market that are surprisingly accurate: DISC, Belbin, Enneagram, Myer-Briggs, 360, etc.

These tools are great allies in the areas of personal development, management development or team diversity management.

Automation and online software make the application of these tools very agile and also very accurate. Many of my clients, who were really skeptical about using these methodologies, were really surprised when they read their reports. They could not imagine that a test of only twenty minutes could extract so much information and so accurate about their way of being.

What do we discover in this exercise of self-knowledge?

When we do this phase of self-knowledge there are different areas that are explored and that serve as the basis for the work that is carried out in the *Leader Development* process.

These are the main points to explore:

- Value it brings to the organization.
- Communication style.
- Areas for improvement.
- Time thieves.
- Strengths.
- Ideal environment.
- Motivators.
- Keys to manage yourself.

Once we have identified your profile and natural leadership style, we can work to adapt your style to each of your collaborators and day-to-day situations.

What is clear is that not all of us are born with innate abilities to lead, but we can always train ourselves to be good leaders. When I work with leaders, the use of these tools not only allows my clients to do a tremendous exercise in self-discovery, but also helps me to tailor processes and strategies so that they can achieve the best results, not only on an individual level but also in their interaction with their team.

HOW TO APPLY ALL THIS IN TEAMS?

These keys and tools can be used not only on a personal level, but also with teams of professionals.

> *Knowing the talents of the members of a team to give each one the mission that best fits his profile and motivators is the best way for the gear to work with the highest performance.*

Each team member will not only achieve better results, but will also be more motivated to do a job that perfectly matches his or her talents.

How can leader self-awareness help in team management?

On repeated occasions I have had clients with serious motivation problems in their teams and they seek help. In many of these cases, part of the problem is that the leadership style that was being applied was not the most appropriate. Other times they have profiles that may be incompatible with someone on their team or even with their boss.

There are no "bad guys" or "good guys" here, but profiles that are so different that they clash, but curiously, they also complement each other.

Many leaders have energetic and challenge-oriented profiles that are great at growing their companies and overcoming obstacles, but when it comes to managing their teams, they can play tricks on them.

Sometimes they are not even aware that their natural leadership style can be counterproductive when they are looking for performance and results.

Every leader has a leadership style that comes naturally to him or her, and this style will probably work very well in certain scenarios. But that same style may not be the most appropriate at other times.

For example, some people tend to delegate, and that style works very well for simple tasks or experienced employees, but will not work as well for someone new to the team. The same is true for someone with a more directive style, which may be ideal for complicated tasks or new employees, but may not work well for someone who lacks motivation.

In other words, we have to identify our natural leadership style and develop those styles that we do not manifest spontaneously but that we can undoubtedly learn and train.

In those cases where I have the self-knowledge report of all the members of the team, the process is even more effective, since it is possible to give much more precise and, therefore, more effective guidelines. Knowing the talents of the members of a team to give each one the mission that best fits their profile and motivators, is the best way for the gear to work with the highest performance.

These self-awareness exercises can help us explain, from a

logical and objective perspective, why we connect better with some team members than with others. Most importantly, we can work on an action plan to achieve better results with those members of our team who are more difficult for us.

Conclusion:

To sum up, it is worth doing the exercise of getting to know ourselves better; the first step to develop ourselves is to know where we need to focus and take actions that will help us grow both personally and professionally.

Aligning functions with the potential of each person, both at the individual and team level, is the best way to achieve high performance and personal satisfaction.

And you, do you already know your best version?

EMOTIONAL INTELLIGENCE

Managers are exposed on a daily basis to difficult, stressful situations that trigger a torrent of emotions, both for them and their teams. Good emotional intelligence can make a difference both in how that situation is perceived and how it is resolved to achieve the best results.

There are even studies that affirm that a good level of emotional intelligence is more relevant to success than IQ.

Findings by Daniel Goleman and the Consortium for Research on Emotional Intelligence in Organizations indicate that emotional intelligence is the most important success factor in any career, more so than IQ or technical expertise.

Emotional intelligence is responsible for 85% to 90% of the success of organizational leaders.

Often my Leadership Development clients request sessions to work on emotional intelligence. They often present me with different situations where they are aware that with greater emotional intelligence they would have solved more effectively many of the difficult situations they have to face in their daily lives. Undoubtedly, a good emotional intelligence has a decisive influence on the success of both our personal and professional life.

Next, I would like to expose different facets of emotional intelligence that have direct application in the day-to-day life of any manager (and, of course, of any person).

What is emotional intelligence?

In principle, emotional intelligence is the ability to recognize and manage emotions effectively. We have to distinguish two facets of emotional intelligence: intrapersonal and interpersonal.

"It is becoming increasingly clear that what really matters when it comes to superior performance in management positions and leaders in large companies is not just their resumes and IQs, but also the way they relate to themselves and others." (Goleman).

Intrapersonal emotional intelligence: that is, the ability to recognize and manage our own emotions. Within this we would distinguish in three parts:

- Self-awareness: knowing how to identify our emotions, recognize our body's response and how we react.
- Self-control: ability to manage our emotions adequately.
- Motivation: ability to generate a positive attitude that helps us to face difficulties in a more effective way.

Interpersonal emotional intelligence: the ability to recognize and interact with the emotions of others. It would comprise two parts:

- Empathy: as the ability to recognize and understand the emotions of others.
- Social skills: such as the ability to interact with others.

The importance of emotional intelligence is on the rise within companies.

How can emotional intelligence help us in our day-to-day work with our teams?

Let's look at five ways emotional intelligence can help us as leaders:

1-Self-awareness: Knowing how to identify our emotions, being aware of how they affect us, our work and our relationship with our team can be crucial. This can help us to know how to detect how we are reaching our limits and act before it is too late. For example, if our weak point when we get stressed are migraines and we detect that we are starting to suffer from them, maybe it is time to start doing something (sport, meditation, etc.) to prevent it from getting worse.

This self-awareness can also help us choose the right time to have a difficult conversation with a colleague. If we are able to recognize that our level of anger or stress may not be appropriate, we will be able to make wiser decisions.

2-Self-management: Have you ever sent an e-mail when you were too angry and then regretted it? So, once you have identified that emotion, it is time to learn how to manage it to prevent it from having negative effects on our productivity and our team. For example, stress and anger are emotions that should be properly managed before they take their toll on us. In addition, emotions are contagious, if we do not manage them properly they can have a negative impact on the team (bad atmosphere, stress, conflicts, talent drain...).

3-Motivation: Being able to generate a positive attitude that helps us to face difficulties in a more effective way is essential, especially when we have a high responsibility and lead a team. There is a proven relationship between productivity and motivation, as I explain in my book *Motivated Teams, Productive Teams.* In addition, positive emotions are also contagious. An enthusiastic and motivated leader will most likely transmit that positivity to his team.

4-Empathy: Being able to detect the emotions of others gives us valuable information that can help us optimize our relationship with others, and of course with our team. Being able to understand their point of view, even when we do not share it, allows us to connect better with them and have much more constructive dialogues.

5-Social skills: A leader must be able to express his opinion in an assertive way, defending his position without offending others. Sometimes we will have to make a criticism, or say 'no', or perhaps manage a conflict. It is important to do this in a way that takes care of our relationship with others. Being assertive does not mean that we cannot have a cordial relationship.

Some people are born with a special ability for all these facets of emotional intelligence. For those who do not have it innately, the good news is that this is something that can be learned and trained.

"Nearly three hundred studies sponsored by different companies underscore that excellence depends more on emotional competencies than on cognitive abilities." (Spencer and Spencer in their book Competence at Work).

THE HABITS OF EXCELLENCE

A few years ago I came across the book *The 7 Habits of Highly Effective People* by Stephen Covey. It coincided precisely with my move to the Netherlands and my new position as Supply Chain Operations Manager.

I used to have the audiobook in the car and I would listen to it over and over again, it was narrated by Stephen Covey himself, and it practically stuck in my marrow. It really marked a before and after for me. I started to apply what I learned and began to see the results. Since then I have not stopped recommending it in my workshops, conferences and in my books. I think that every leader should know these principles, so I could not fail to dedicate one of the chapters of this book to it.

These are the habits Covey describes:

First habit: Be proactive.

Being proactive means taking responsibility for your own life and exercising the ability to select your response to any event. This implies behaving according to your conscious decision, based on your values, not on the conditions in which you find yourself. In conclusion: it is not what happens to us, but what we do with what happens to us.

Second habit: Start with an end in mind.

This habit of effectiveness reflects personal leadership and fully satisfies the need to find meaning in one's existence and to begin each day with a clear understanding of one's desired direction and destination. This habit has to do with setting goals, short, medium and long term. Establish our mission and vision.

Third habit: Do first things first.

Stephen Covey said that every activity can be classified according to two criteria: 1) Urgency, those activities that require immediate action. 2) Importance, those activities that have to do with results. Thus, each activity is susceptible to be classified in the following quadrants:

1) Urgent and important: Crisis management.
2) Non-urgent and important: Proactive management.
3) Urgent and not important: Reactive administration.
4) Not urgent and not important: Ineffective administration.

It is obvious that it is the second quadrant that is key to achieving effectiveness.

Fourth habit: Think win-win.

This habit of effectiveness exemplifies mutual benefit and helps powerfully to find balance in human relationships with a sense of common good and fairness. This is the habit that enables the achievement of shared satisfactions among all those involved in a negotiation process. This model represents mutually satisfactory benefits, in addition to the fact that it involves reciprocal learning and mutual influence. The history of conflicts in all psychological and social spheres reflects the absence of this understanding, first, and the unfortunate practice of negotiations, later.

Fifth habit: Seek first to understand and then to be understood.

This is the habit that supports the need to empathetically understand the other person in order to be understood and then be able to build more constructive interpersonal relationships. This habit especially emphasizes the importance of empathic listening in the process of human communication. Although all habits of effectiveness are closely related to emotional intelligence, this habit is to a greater degree because of its own emotional connotations.

Sixth habit: Look for synergies.

This is the habit that underlies the synergic achievements of teamwork, that is, of those teams in which the result of the collective is greater than the simple sum of its members. It could also be said that the IQ of the team is greater than the average IQ of those who participate in its composition.

Seventh habit: Sharpen the saw.

This habit of effectiveness interprets continuous improvement and self-renewal, the basic maintenance necessary to keep the remaining habits working properly, offers a horizon of personal improvement in each and every area of our personality. This is the habit that allows us to understand personal improvement in the physical, mental, socioemotional and spiritual dimensions. In any case, the lack of a proper renewal in these dimensions can have a high cost for people.

Eighth habit: From effectiveness to greatness.

The eighth habit was published in a later book, but it contributes as much as the previous ones. This habit involves listening to our own "inner voice" and teaching others to identify their own. It is about teaching others the art of making the most of what is unique to each individual, so that each person becomes indispensable in the organization by virtue of his or her unique capabilities. In other words, it is a habit that helps the leader to empower each and every member of his team.

In this book you will see how these habits are very present. I personally think they are the foundation for healthy and motivating leadership and for achieving excellence both personally and professionally.

STRESS MANAGEMENT AND BURNOUT

I had a tough time when I started working in the Netherlands and managing teams for the first time. I was in charge of moving and setting up the European production department for a big company. It brought a mix of challenges that really tested me:

- First time with managing a team.
- A new position with a significant increase in my responsibilities (from Product Engineer to Supply Chain Operations Manager).
- 80% of my team was new to their positions.
- Relocation to a new country (from Ireland to The Netherlands).
- International relocation of an entire Supply Chain department.
- Remote location with respect to the rest of the company, which made it more difficult to receive the necessary support from my boss and the rest of the organization.
- Etc, etc, etc, etc...

To sum up, a situation that brought me to the brink of burnout and, at the same time, provided me with an enormous learning experience.

Managers often carry a significant workload. They are generally expected not only to manage their teams, but also to attend to their own tasks. Therefore, anyone managing a team has additional stress, as they have more interactions, more responsibilities and more pressures.

In addition, managers face other difficulties. They are often under pressure from above and from below, i.e. their superiors are demanding and their team is also putting a lot of pressure on them, and this can be overwhelming. They are faced with a large number of new tasks that they often do not know how to prioritize, and sometimes they can become totally exhausted. This often results in high levels of stress, which can affect their productivity and can even lead to time off work.

Many managers who lead a team for the first time have gone from flowing with their previous jobs, to seeming stagnant.

This can generate in these professionals emotions such as frustration, stress, blockages, and even fear, which they are unable to control and which can lead to negative consequences, both for them and for their team, and ultimately, their company.

Result: your daily workday becomes a hell full of stress, lack of time, excessive workload, and with a lot of pressure (demands, complaints and problems to attend to) both from your team and from your superiors.

Burnout can have a major impact, not only on middle management, but also on the motivation of your people and the company's bottom line.

In addition, emotions are contagious. Just as an inspirational leader can create positive change in the workplace, a burned-out and exhausted manager can have a very negative effect on his or her team.

Learning how to manage this new situation can prevent burnout and its negative consequences. This should be one of the priorities in any organization.

The World Health Organization (WHO) has recently given the deserved prominence to burnout or "burnout syndrome", which it defines as a recognized disease with its own entity, a major breakthrough in a society where it seems that the feared negative effects of stress in the world of work are beginning to be recognized.

The list in which it is included, compiled by the WHO, is based on the conclusions of medical experts from around the world, who met in 2019 in Geneva as part of the organization's World Assembly. For the first time, professional burnout enters this ranking of the greatest threats to our health.

Spain, and according to the National Survey of Working Conditions prepared in 2015, 13.8% of respondents answered that they always experience stress at work; 15.8%, almost always; and 35.9%, sometimes.

IS STRESS THE SAME AS BURNOUT?

There is a direct relationship between stress and productivity. Moderate levels of stress can even be positive in increasing productivity. However, excessive stress and burnout are always negative.

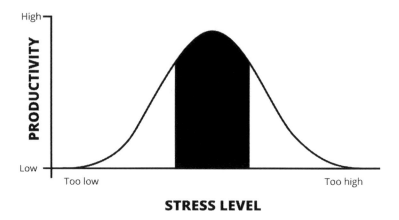

STRESS LEVEL

Burnout and excessive stress have negative consequences at the individual level. Some of the negative effects that we can find can be:

- Errors in the work performed.
- Difficulty in making decisions.
- Deterioration of personal relationships.
- Lack of concentration.
- Sleep disorders.
- Physical and mental health problems.
- Etc...

In addition to the negative consequences at the individual level, stress and burnout also have an impact on team and company performance:

- Sick leave.
- Absenteeism.

- Increase in occupational accidents.
- Lower customer satisfaction.
- Conflicts.
- Decrease in productivity.
- Leakage of talent.
- Etc...

Let's take a look at the main symptoms and differences according to the *Expansión* article, "Estar quemado ya es una enfermedad oficialmente" (July 3, 2019).

STRESS	BURNOUT
Over-involvement in problems.	Lack of involvement and disengagement.
Emotional hyperactivity.	Emotional dullness.
The physiological damage is primary.	The emotional damage is primary.
Exhaustion or lack of physical energy.	Burnout affects motivation and psychic energy.
Depression as a symptom to maintain physical energy.	It is similar to a loss of reference ideals, sadness.
May have positive effects in moderate exposures.	It only produces negative effects.

WHAT CAUSES STRESS IN THE LEADER?

The team we lead. Leading a team is one of the most complex tasks any professional can have. The members of the team itself not only involve time and dedication, but are also a

source of interruptions, demands, complaints, conflicts, etc....
This undoubtedly puts enormous pressure on your leader.

Excessive demands and responsibilities. A certain level of challenge is needed to maintain focus and motivation, as well as to develop new skills, although it is important that the demands do not exceed one's limits. This factor can be directly linked to positions that have a poorly defined profile, excessive amounts of work and skills that are not compatible with those required by the position.

Imbalance between effort and reward. Putting in too much effort without satisfying the need for a reward can turn into job stress. Reward can come in many different forms, such as helping others, recognition, increased knowledge, personal growth or monetary compensation.

Not being in control. Some of the common causes of stress at work include complaints about having too much responsibility with too little authority. The ideal is to have a good balance between responsibilities and personal control.

Organizational change. Organizational change can be defined as any change in people, structure, technology or processes. Organizational change varies in degree and direction, which can generate uncertainty and can create both stress and opportunities.

The boss. One of the most common reasons for stress includes lack of support from managers or supervisors. It can also happen that a manager who is under the effects of excessive stress passes it on to his or her team. Other times it may be character incompatibility that can trigger tensions.

Lack of support. A supportive environment is one where managers provide clear and consistent information and co-workers and the team are ready to help. When a manager feels that his or her boss does not support him or her, it can be very frustrating and stressful. If that lack of support is widespread within the team he or she is leading, the source of the problem should be analyzed and it should be a priority to fix it.

Change of position and responsibility. Change always costs, even if it is for the better and even if it is something we asked for. It can be very stressful to be granted a promotion, which often involves an increase in workload and responsibilities. This can be a lot of effort and pressure.

Lack of work-life balance. Many managers often face long working hours that prevent them from having a healthy balance between their professional and personal lives. This often takes its toll in the medium to long term.

WHAT CAN WE DO TO PREVENT OR MANAGE EXCESSIVE STRESS?

These are twelve keys that can help prevent states of excessive stress both in ourselves and in our teams:

Key 1: Reasonable goals and objectives should follow the SMART format (specific, measurable, achievable, relevant, time-bound).

Key 2: Profile-position matching, this requires knowing our skills and those of each of our collaborators, and that they are compatible with those required by the position.

Key 3: Recognition and reward at work is the return for an employee's dedication and effort at work. This recognition must be deserved, sincere and well dosed over time.

Key 4: Participation and empowerment, i.e., creating an environment in which people have an impact on the decisions and actions that affect their work, and employees have a degree of autonomy and responsibility to make decisions regarding their specific tasks within the organization.

Key 5: Conflict management and prevention by promoting emotional intelligence and assertiveness.

Key 6: A good development plan, to detect both needs that our team may have to be able to perform their work well, as well as professional development aspirations.

Key 7: Foster an environment of trust in the team that promotes positive working relationships and confronts inappropriate behaviors; this also promotes productivity and employee commitment.

Key 8: Flexible schedules and work-life balance can go a long way in preventing and relieving stressful situations.

Key 9: Healthy and motivating leadership, so that the manager or supervisor is not a source of stress but the opposite, i.e., a support to drive the team.

Key 10: Promote a healthy lifestyle, such as encouraging the use of bicycles to go to work, healthy diet, exercise, rest, etc...

Key 11: Encouraging practices such as mindfulness or emotional intelligence in the work environment can help to relativize difficult situations, improve concentration, maintain calm and prevent states of anxiety.

Key 12: Time and priority management techniques can help, and help a lot, to regain control of the situation and therefore, to avoid stress accumulation.

HOW CAN A COMPANY PREVENT BURNOUT AMONG ITS MIDDLE MANAGERS AND EXECUTIVES?

According to Fastcompany, managers can be provided with training and coaching, so that they can perform their mission while minimizing the risk of burnout. These are the five keys to keep in mind:

1. Start your training as soon as possible
From the moment a manager is promoted, they should be prepared for it, so as to increase their ability to cope and reduce their stress levels and risk of burnout. To this end, a development plan should be ensured that takes into account the training and coaching they need to manage all the challenges they face.

Many companies invest heavily in the training of senior managers, but neglect the development of middle management without giving them the importance they deserve. They are key players in any organization.

2. Training and development adapted to your needs
It is crucial that the training and education that is carried out with managers is really up to their needs. It is essential that you address the issues they really need. It is a matter of assessing their needs and developing a realistic and effective development plan.

The most frequently requested topics are: leadership, team management, effective communication, conflict management, time management and productivity...

On the other hand, the format is important, so that it fits their workload and their schedule, and is delivered in a flexible and tailor-made way. In-company training programs are ideal for all of this.

3. Take advantage of new technologies

In some cases, other formats could be considered, such as individual *Leadership Development* programs or even online training that allow the professional to organize his or her training where and how it best suits his or her schedule.

Harvard Business Publishing research shows that most business leaders tend to be very familiar with common web-based communications platforms such as Zoom, WebEx, GoToMeeting and Skype. So why not leverage these technologies in middle management training and development?

It's a great opportunity. Technology can help break down the time barrier and allow them to defuse burnout issues by helping them squeeze in learning when and where the opportunity arises.

4. Helping middle management to be true leaders

Becoming a manager often involves a significant change in mindset, requiring a paradigm shift from "personal achievement" to success based on "team achievement".
Just a few months ago, when I was talking to a Human Resources Director about the needs of his middle managers, he told me that, when it came to giving instructions to his teams,

especially when it came to uncomfortable orders, they avoided responsibility, hiding behind the fact that "they are orders that come from above", when in fact what they are looking for is that they take the reins, and exercise the authority and responsibility that their position requires. That is to say, that they really assume that they are leaders who must exercise their authority.

This does not mean that they have to dictate orders, but that they are able to provide healthy and motivating leadership that inspires their teams to do what is expected of them.

However, in flat organizations, middle management may not exercise much formal authority to control the actions of that team.

Being responsible for results without having the power to make those results happen? That's the best way to get burned out.

You can reduce the risk of burnout by ensuring that you equip middle managers with a leadership mindset that enables them to establish trust, generate motivation and build a positive team culture. With the right approach, middle managers can get the results they need through persuasion and collaboration.

5. Developing leaders beyond classroom training

In 2011, three Harvard Business School professors published The *Handbook for Teaching Leadership: Knowing, Doing and Being*. The book made a persuasive case for why leadership development depends as much on practicing leadership (doing) and changing mindsets (being) as it does on the traditional practice of acquiring new ideas (knowing). This argument was so compelling that Harvard Business School redesigned its own MBA program to deliver the whole *Knowing-Doing-Being* package.

How can you apply know-how-to-be principles to your own leadership development program? The greatest impact is achieved by combining practical on-the-job application with real situations (and real teams), classroom coaching and experience sharing with other managers in similar situations. This helps to break out of the stress and burnout trap by replacing it with a positive feedback loop and continuous improvement.

> *"Want even better results? Have managers go through the group training program to create a sense of togetherness. They will build lasting relationships with their peers and establish connections that will ultimately strengthen collaboration throughout your company."*
> *(Peter Walsh, senior director of global marketing at Harvard Business Publishing).*

For this reason, In Company training, with the middle management team, has such a positive effect on organizations, helping them to share experiences not only in the classroom but also when applying the learning in their day-to-day work, which allows them to follow up, consolidate learning and improve the results they achieve when putting it into practice with their teams.

It is worthwhile to review all these points with the management and middle management team, not only to prevent excessive stress and burnout, but also to improve the well-being and productivity of our teams. Where are you going to start?

LEARNING FROM MISTAKES

I remember the case of a manager who, despite having a very successful career with excellent results in the company where he worked, one day made a major mistake, a mistake with a tremendous cost for the company.

The higher the level of responsibility within the company, the greater the consequences of an error.

It had such an enormous impact that the management decided to fire this person. A difficult and painful decision, because this person, who had contributed a lot of value to the company in the past, but the dimension of the consequences of this oversight justified it. The fact is that, when they were meeting to deliver the letter of dismissal, the CEO told him: *"You know, I think that with this mistake and everything that has happened, you have learned as much or more than in any master's degree from the best business school. So it would be a shame not to take advantage of all that knowledge and experience now."* He then tore up the letter of dismissal. Thus began a second chance. In time, it proved to be the right decision.

It is clear that the higher the level of responsibility within the company, the greater the consequences of a mistake. Therefore, as we advance and grow professionally, error and failure management becomes more important.

In addition, when we lead a team, it is important to instill a good culture of error management so that mistakes are dealt with constructively. When this is not done, the moment someone makes a mistake, they will try to hide it, lie about it, or worse, blame it on someone else. The responsibility of assuming that mistake is avoided and the environment becomes toxic.

If we want to cultivate true healthy and motivating leadership, we must be the first to lead by example and show that we assume our own mistakes. This is what we should also expect from our team.

It is not a matter of not falling into the mistake, but of getting up and learning how to emerge stronger from it.

When faced with a failure or a mistake, it is important to take advantage of the occasion and turn it into a great learning opportunity.

This does not mean that we are going to encourage people to make mistakes. The fewer mistakes, the better, but we do have to manage them correctly. We have to own them, take responsibility, solve them and take preventive measures so that we don't trip over the same stone again.

It's all about drawing conclusions and learning. How do you do that? Let's look at the steps to learn from those falls:

Step 1- Repair the damage: The most urgent thing to do is to do everything possible to correct the mistake and its possible negative consequences. In some situations this can become really urgent and we need to take immediate action. This requires more immediacy in time even than looking for the person responsible for the mistake.

Step 2- Self-criticism: If we have been responsible, we must be able to see where we have been wrong, in a spirit of self-criticism, but always with a constructive approach. It is important to recognize our mistake and assume it, but at the same time not to let this affect our self-esteem or let feelings of guilt arise that do not help us to improve the situation.

Step 3- Analysis: We must explore all possibilities, with perspective and with a view to better prepare ourselves for the next time. What could we have done differently? Were there other alternatives? If we were faced with the same situation again, what would we change?

Step 4- Learnings: Not only do we have to analyze what we have learned from this experience, but we must also be able to detect those skills or knowledge that we are lacking in order to do better next time. We must also be able to detect those skills or knowledge that we lack in order to do better next time. Do I need to acquire a new skill? Do I need to learn something new to help me do better?

Step 5- Action plan: Once we have explored the previous steps, it is time to do something about it, to proactively get down to work. What is the next step? What am I going to do so that it doesn't happen again?

*It is not a matter of not falling, but of getting
up and learning to emerge stronger from it.*

All this applies to you as an individual as well as to your team. I hope that from now on you will see those mistakes in a more positive light, and turn them into an opportunity to learn, improve and become stronger. Instill this culture in your team and lead by example.

SHARPEN THE SAW

This is neither more nor less than the seventh habit of Stephen Covey's book. A habit that sometimes is not given the importance it has and is even forgotten.

Before I continue, I would like to share a story that helps to better understand this concept:

Once upon a time, two woodcutters went into the forest to cut wood; one of them, large and strong, began to cut with great eagerness, without resting for a single minute. The other, a little smaller, began to cut wood, but unlike his companion, he stopped every few minutes. At the end of the day, the first of them, who had stopped practically for nothing, looked up and saw that his companion's pile of firewood was considerably larger than his own. All indignant and perplexed, he went to him and said: "How can it be that you have cut more wood than me, if you have been stopping practically every hour? His companion replied: "Quite simply, because every time I stopped it was to sharpen the saw".

And how do we sharpen our saw? Our mind and body are the best and most important tools at our disposal. It is important that both are in good shape to face difficulties and challenges.

"Sharpening the saw" consists of dedicating time precisely to the maintenance of these tools. On the one hand, taking care of our mind, our personal development, never stop learning, training, reading books that inspire us and bring us closer to our goals. I consider training so important that I dedicate a whole chapter of this book to it.

Lately, practices such as mindfulness and meditation are becoming a growing trend in the Western world, even reaching the corporate world. However, these practices are nothing new; they were already part of the routine of Buddhist monks more than two thousand years ago. What is new is that it is only now that the benefits they can bring us have been scientifically proven, to increase our concentration and even prevent states of depression or anxiety.

Many times we are so busy in our daily routine that we do not stop to "sharpen the saw", without realizing that it is an investment of our time in something that in the end will make us more productive.

On the other hand, we have to take care of our body, probably the most important tool we have. To do so, it is important to take care of our diet, our sleep, to exercise regularly. In short, to take care of ourselves. Our body has to last us a lifetime.

When we take care of our body, we improve our health and energy level. In addition, if we look good physically, it can increase our self-esteem and self-confidence. That will affect our performance positively and the energy we radiate.

At the company level it is also necessary to "sharpen the saw", training our teams, working on leadership, promoting teamwork and, in short, taking care of all those aspects that can make the difference between achieving high performance or not.

As a leader, you are sharpening your saw right now by reading this book, you are cultivating your leadership knowledge and skills, which will help you perform better in your day-to-day life.

In conclusion, set aside time in your schedule for everything that helps you take care of yourself and be more productive. We tend to downplay its importance and let other issues hijack our attention, time and energy.

If we make sure to reserve time in our agenda for these types of activities, we will avoid them being left undone.

This does not mean that we cannot have some flexibility. An example: Imagine that you decide to reserve every Monday, Wednesday and Friday, from 20.00 to 21.00h to exercise, and one day you have a work trip or any other unforeseen event. You can decide to move that exercise time to a Tuesday or Thursday or to a different time of the day. In other words, you find another time for it, but you don't erase it from your schedule. Whereas if we don't make sure we reserve these slots in the calendar, we will always find a reason to keep postponing it indefinitely, and that's the best way we will never do it.

Believe me, this is a great investment. You will have to dedicate some of your time to it, but it will pay off with increased productivity and health both physically and mentally.

When was the last time you stopped to "sharpen the saw"?

NEVER STOP LEARNING

Some time ago I read an article in *Equiposytalento.com* that left me perplexed. It stated that during 2016 there were 67% of Spanish companies that did not carry out any training programmed and subsidized with the available funds (also known as Tripartita or Fundae). Moreover, not even 50% of the budget that the State had available in 2016 for the training of employed workers was spent. With these data, it is worth making the general reflection about whether corporate training in Spain is really betting on.

Knowing that many companies could finance 100% of the cost of training using their credits and that, moreover, if they are not used, they are lost from one year to the next, I keep asking myself why they do not take advantage of them? Is it due to ignorance or laziness?

Taking care of our training and that of our teams is of crucial importance, both for the company's results and for the motivation of its employees.

Many may think that training is a waste of time, others may even think why invest in employees who may end up leaving the company? This mentality is far from correct.

Within the development plan, which each employee should have as part of their annual performance evaluation, we should find out what their training needs are in order to be able to perform their job better.

Training our teams is a win-win situation, the employee wins and the company wins.

Benefits for companies:

- Better adaptation of companies to changes in the environment.
- It favors the incorporation of new technologies, as well as new management and organizational systems.
- It helps to consolidate and transmit the company's culture, values and mission.
- Add value to your workforce, with better trained and qualified workers.
- Increases productivity and company performance.
- Improves the company's level of competitiveness.
- Increases the quality of products and/or services.
- It allows for greater flexibility and adaptability of the workforce.
- Increases employee engagement, satisfaction and motivation.
- It favors talent retention and internal promotion.

Employee benefits:

- They acquire new knowledge, skills and abilities.
- Facilitates professional development.
- Increases employee motivation as they see that the company invests in their development.

- It makes it possible to keep abreast of new technologies and ways of working.
- Promotes growth within the company.
- Improve the level of efficiency in your area.
- Improves efficient decision making and problem solving.

Personally I have the great satisfaction that my clients are companies that care about providing their teams with the training they need to keep progressing and improving every day. A great success that translates into more motivated and productive teams.

LEADERSHIP DEVELOPMENT TRAINING

There are currently multiple options for leadership training.

Leadership Development guides managers to discover their strengths in order to organize an action plan to overcome potential obstacles in their leadership and increase their value to the organization.

In this section I am going to talk about what I know first hand, that is, the options I offer to my clients. When I work with my clients I combine personal development, mentoring and training in sessions tailored to the needs of each company.

Different modalities can be chosen:

- **In Company group training sessions,** with the company's management team in their own facilities. They can be face-to-face or webinar type.

- **Individualized *Leadership Development*** are customized trainings that consist of video-conference sessions (via Skype or similar) designed to measure, where specific topics of the leader and his team are combined and treated in a 100% personalized way.

- **Online training.** This option consists of online courses that can be followed in a flexible way, adapting to any schedule. The lessons are distributed in short videos that are easy to include in your daily routine. It allows you to develop your leadership wherever and however you want, with total flexibility.

- **Premium Leadership Development Program.** A very complete form of leadership development that combines the two previous options. Probably the most complete program on the market to guide executives and middle managers in the leadership of high performance teams in a personalized, flexible and effective way, combining the benefits of individual sessions and online training with excellent results.

The executive who follows this accompaniment becomes a more efficient professional by modifying his or her management style and optimizing his or her attitudes as a leader.

Especially indicated in situations where it is desired to achieve:

- Development of leadership skills.
- Facing career or personal changes.
- Ensure success after a promotion or new competencies required.
- Reduction of stress levels

- Learn to delegate, to manage risk more effectively.
- More efficient time management and increased productivity.
- Learn to communicate more effectively.
- Increase emotional intelligence.
- Increased efficiency in problem solving and decision making.

BENEFITS:

The benefits for managers who underwent *Leadership Development* processes improved in:

- Working relationships with direct subordinates (reported by 77% of executives).
- Working relationships with immediate supervisors (71%).
- Teamwork (67%).
- Working relationships with colleagues (63%).
- Job satisfaction (61%).
- Reduction of conflicts (52%).
- Organizational commitment (44%).
- Working relationships with customers (37%).

A study conducted by the firm Manchester Inc. All participants underwent coaching programs aimed at improving performance for a period of six to twelve months. Respondents were 100 executives from successful companies (mostly FORTUNE 1000).

Conclusion:

In summary, despite the potential costs, training and development provides both the employee and the organization with benefits that make this investment in resources and time worthwhile.

PART 2:

SOCIAL INTELLIGENCE
OF THE LEADER

- SOCIAL SKILLS
- THE IMPORTANCE OF ACTIVE LISTENING
- DIFFICULT CONVERSATIONS
- CONFLICT MANAGEMENT
- KEYS TO MANAGE YOUR BOSS
- KEYS TO BUILDING TRUST
- PERSONAL BRANDING AND NETWORKING

SOCIAL SKILLS

According to Goleman, social intelligence is a person's ability to relate to others in an empathetic and assertive manner. It helps us to communicate effectively, to know how to manage our emotions properly and to obtain a good result as a product of our social interactions. Emotional intelligence is closely linked to social intelligence, since both include the proper management of your emotions to improve your interpersonal relationships.

Any professional leading a team should keep in mind that they are working with people, so their social intelligence, social and communication skills are of crucial importance. These leaders must be able to achieve productivity through their team.

Being firm does not mean that we cannot have a cordial relationship.

A leader must express his opinion in an assertive way by defending his position without offending others. Sometimes we will have to make a criticism, or say 'no', or perhaps manage a conflict. It is important to do this in a way that takes care of our relationship with our team members.

HOW TO APPLY SOFT SKILLS IN THE LEADERSHIP OF OUR TEAMS?

Smile. We should practice smiling more. Did you know that simply smiling helps us feel better? Smiling at others also makes us receive a more positive response from our co-workers. Give it a try! The next time you address someone on your team, do it with a smile, and notice the response from others.

Active listening. While talking to your employees, make sure you are fully attentive during the conversation, and give them enough time to express their opinion. When conversing with them, put their needs first. When your employee feels listened to, the quality of that conversation improves tremendously, as does the leader-employee relationship.

Communicate assertively. That is, defending our position or opinion while respecting others and at the same time making ourselves respected. We can learn to make difficult requests or to say 'no' in a way that does not damage our relationship with others and that achieves our objectives.

Give and receive constructive criticism. It is important that when we give feedback we do it in a way that it is not received as an attack. Correcting what is necessary within our teams can be done without creating discomfort. At other times we will be the ones to receive the criticism, it is also something that we must learn to manage properly.

Build trust. Without trust, a team cannot function effectively. A good leader is a fundamental piece in the generation of trust within a team, and it is essential that this exists so that there is cooperation between each of its members. Make sure you do this.

Manage and prevent conflicts. Whenever there is a group of people working together, disagreements can arise. That is why it is very important, as leaders, to have the ability to manage these situations that can sometimes be really uncomfortable and hinder the good performance of a team. There will be times when, even if we are not part of a conflict, our mediation can help the situation to be resolved in a constructive way.

Empathy. Being able to detect the emotions of others gives us valuable information that can help us optimize our relationship with our team. Being able to understand their point of view, even when we do not share it, allows us to better connect with them and establish much more constructive dialogues.

Deal constructively with problems. If there are work-related problems with some of your co-workers, talk openly with them, tell them how you feel and what you expect them to do. This is about giving constructive feedback and preventing the problem from escalating or recurring. Sometimes, when we get carried away by impulsive reactions, we can take actions that we may regret later.

Inspire enthusiasm. Intelligent optimism will help to generate positive thoughts that will give rise to positive emotions that, in turn, trigger certain behaviors or actions that will give certain results. So we will be much more likely to have positive results the more positive the thought that generated it. Remember, emotions are contagious, both the good ones and the limiting ones.

In the past, tasks were done by imposing authority, nowadays leaders have to be able to influence their team.

Some people are born with a special facility for developing good social skills. For those who do not have them innately, the good news is that this is something that can be learned and trained. In this book we will review formulas for doing this more effectively.

THE IMPORTANCE OF ACTIVE LISTENING

One of the skills that every leader must have is the ability to communicate effectively with his or her team; well, in this process active listening plays a crucial role.

Often, when others speak, we are thinking about our response instead of trying to understand what the other person is communicating.

Sometimes, it seems like we are listening, but our minds are somewhere else.

At other times, however, we appear to be distracted by other things and in reality we have perfectly understood the message.

In none of these cases could we be considered to be practicing active listening.

The ability to listen to our team is undoubtedly one of the qualities that every leader must cultivate.

WHAT IS ACTIVE LISTENING?

My concept of active listening consists of meeting two conditions, both of which are necessary:

1st Condition: Hearing and understanding the message that the other party has communicated to us.
2nd Condition: To make our interlocutor feel heard, that is, to show that we have heard and understood his message.

Certain people are innately capable of active listening. It is an extraordinary quality, since the quality of their conversations is enormous and they make their interlocutors feel very good, which positively impacts their personal relationships.

Fortunately, there are techniques that help us improve our listening, and in my experience, they really work.

A few years ago I discovered, thanks to a self-awareness report, that I needed to improve my listening. As soon as I became aware of this area for improvement, I firmly set out to learn how I should actively listen and to practice what I had learned.

At first we have to practice these techniques consciously, making an effort, but if we persevere we can internalize these skills and finally manifest them in a natural and sincere way.

HOW CAN I ACHIEVE GOOD ACTIVE LISTENING?

Here are some keys to keep in mind if we want to improve our listening skills.

Some techniques that can help us to achieve a better understanding and connection with the interlocutor are the following:

TYPE	INTENT	EXAMPLE
Clarify	For additional data.	Can you clarify this for me...? What do you mean...? Specifically ...?
Paraphrase	To check that our interpretation is correct and show that we are listening.	If I understand correctly what you are saying is that....
Neutral	Simply to imply that we follow what we are told.	I see. How interesting.
Empathy	Show that we are able to put ourselves in their place. It does not mean agreeing with the other person's position.	I understand what you feel... I notice that...
Summarize	Make a compilation of the most important points we have heard.	These are the main ideas of what you tell me....

Non-verbal language when listening

Body language will be our ally in making our interlocutor feel heard.

Here are some details to keep in mind:

-Visual contact, but without discomfort.
-Physical closeness and slightly forward leaning posture.
-Facial expression of interest in the conversation.
-Nodding.
-Reflect in our face the emotion of the other.
-Smile (only if appropriate for the occasion!).

We must not forget the power of silence, letting the other person speak and not interrupting until he/she has finished greatly improves the quality of the dialogue.

If we practice these techniques with our interlocutors, we will see how we gradually improve our listening skills, and communication with our team will improve as a result.

How about you? How do you listen?

DIFFICULT CONVERSATIONS

Throughout our personal and professional lives we are sometimes confronted with conversations that can be particularly difficult for us and where our personal and sometimes even professional relationship with others is at stake.

This becomes even more evident when we have to lead a team, where the way we communicate with them becomes especially important to achieve the results we are looking for.

Here are some guidelines that can help us in the most common uncomfortable conversations that we may encounter in our daily lives.

KEYS TO GIVE CONSTRUCTIVE CRITICISM TO YOUR TEAM

Constructive feedback is very necessary when we want to correct some behavior or task of our team, that is, to point out situations in which someone does something that is not the most appropriate or that is not giving results.

Giving good quality feedback can have a very powerful motivational effect.

It is essential to indicate this as soon as possible, so that it is corrected immediately and does not become an even bigger problem. It is very important how we are going to offer this feedback, so that it is constructive and is not interpreted as an attack.

To do so, let's look at the key points to take into account when making a critique:

Choose the right place. It is not the same to criticize in an open space where other colleagues can hear it as it is to do it in private. The intention is not to make our collaborator uncomfortable, but to give him constructive feedback that will help him to work better and become a better professional.

Choose the right moment. It is not the same to offer criticism when someone is relaxed and receptive as when that person is in a bad mood, under pressure or in a situation that could make that feedback counterproductive. Sometimes it is better to let the situation calm down before acting. Waiting for the right moment can make the difference between the success or failure of that criticism.

Describe the behavior that bothers you without labeling or rejecting the person, it is important not to attack the identity of the interlocutor. In other words, do not criticize what the person "is", but what he or she "does". It is not the same to say "you are informal" as to say "you have delivered your report two days late". Do you see the difference?

Explain how you feel so that the other person understands the consequences of what he or she is doing. There are times when someone does what they do without being aware of the effect it has on others.

Be based on facts. Be specific by giving examples and data, if we give a superficial and generalized criticism you may not get to understand what you have to correct. Let's be specific about what you did, when you did it, how you did it, who it impacted, and all the data that can help describe the problem.

Ask clearly what you want the other person to do differently, it is important to be specific in how you expect them to act from now on and how they can fix it.

Explain the consequences of both doing and not doing it (positive and negative). Make it clear what are the reasons that have led you to make that criticism and its effects.

Assertiveness. We will first and foremost ask for what we want, but always with respect. We will be direct and clear, but always careful not to hurt the other person's feelings.

Criticizing well, giving this constructive feedback, helps our team members to grow. In short, it helps them to know where they have to row, we are giving them information on how they can achieve the team's objectives.

It is important that we not only give constructive feedback, we also need to recognize a job well done.

It is when we maintain this balance (recognition/constructive criticism) that we will achieve the motivational effect I mentioned earlier. When are you going to apply it?

SANDWICH TECHNIQUE FOR GIVING FEEDBACK OR MAKING REQUESTS

This technique works especially well for giving feedback or for making requests that may be somewhat uncomfortable. It works not only in a professional setting, but in any environment where we communicate with other people.

It is about making that request or criticism that may be uncomfortable in a way that the other person is more receptive and, at the same time, does not interpret it as a personal or negative attack.

The name of this technique, 'sandwich', is a metaphor. When we have a sandwich, the first layer is a slice of bread, soft. Then there is a layer with what really matters in the sandwich, the filling, the consistent part. Finally, the last layer is another slice of bread, soft.

This is precisely the structure of this message:

STEP 1: A first "soft" layer that helps to capture the attention and receptiveness of our interlocutor, an empathic phrase that helps us to connect and where we describe the behavior of the other person showing a positive and understanding attitude. It could be verbalized as: *"I understand that you... (describe the other's behavior with empathy)"*.

STEP 2: Next we would start with the second layer, the strong part of the message, what we really want to ask or tell him/her. This is the moment to say how we feel, what bothers us or what we want them to do for us, being direct and clear, but at the same time respectful. We could use phrases like:

"When you do that I... (add your own reasons by saying how you feel)."

"What I would like you to do is... (proposed solution that can satisfy both of you)."

STEP 3: Finally, the soft layer at the end, where we want to leave a good taste in the mouth and avoid leaving the other person with a negative feeling. Here would be the moment to show our appreciation and to highlight the positive consequences if they do what we are asking them to do. It could be verbalized as: *"Then .... (thanks and positive consequences)"*.

> **Example:** *I understand that you like to listen to loud music. But when you do, I feel irritable and can't do my job well. How about turning down the volume or using headphones? I would be really grateful if you would and we could work much better together.*

KEYS TO RECEIVE CRITICISM IN AN ASSERTIVE WAY

In the same way that we can correct others by offering our feedback and consider it as something necessary and constructive, we must be prepared to receive it from others, whether they are collaborators, superiors, clients, etc...
Receiving criticism is not something that pleases or is

comfortable, but we must reframe ourselves to take advantage of this information and turn it into an opportunity for improvement. It is very important how we are going to receive that feedback: whether it is constructive and not interpreted as an attack will depend largely on us.

To this end, we will look at the key points to take into account when receiving a critique:

- **Show empathy:** Regardless of whether we agree or not, we should try to put ourselves in their shoes and try to understand how they feel and what has led them to criticize us. We can verbalize this with expressions such as: *I understand how you feel....*

- **Ask for information with details, examples and data.** It is important that we ask for all the information necessary to understand what the problem really is and that we do not make our own misinterpretation. Asking for details, examples and data to help us identify what we have not done right is critical. The first step to fixing something is to know what needs to be fixed.

- **Look at how to improve that behavior.** Once we have all the details, it's a matter of analyzing what we can do about it. Is it something we can improve? Do we want to change it?

- **See if they could be right in some way**. It is also important to recognize our mistakes in case we have made a mistake. This is a gesture of maturity and responsibility. If, on the other hand, we are absolutely sure that we have acted correctly, we should argue our reasons, always in an assertive way. That is to say, defending our position while maintaining respect for the other.

- **Find out what the other wants you to do differently or how to fix it**. This point is crucial. We must never ignore what we have to do to solve the problem. We have to check what the other person really expects from us. Sometimes we may take actions with the best will to solve the problem, but despite our efforts, they do not go in the direction of what is really expected of us.

- **Distinguish between constructive criticism and attempts at manipulation.** When in doubt, always try to take criticism positively, as important information for improvement. If they cannot give you clear examples or data to help you improve, it may be an attempt at manipulation.

How did you react the last time you received criticism? Would you change anything in that reaction?

KEYS TO SAY 'NO' ASSERTIVELY

For some people, one of the most uncomfortable situations is when they have to say 'no' to someone. In fact, saying 'no' is not a bad thing. What is bad is not being able to say it when the occasion calls for it.

In my time management workshops I frequently meet people whose main problem is to embark on countless tasks that do not bring them closer to their goals. That is, tasks that keep them busy, day after day, make them focus on the short term and as a consequence they lose perspective and, even worse, drain their time and energy.

Very often they are tasks that they embark on because they don't know how to say 'no' in time. As Steve Jobs used to say:

Only by learning to say 'no' can we focus on the things that really matter.

When they raise the problem, they tell me that they have a hard time refusing to do what others ask them to do, for fear of damaging a personal relationship. But how to avoid this?

In reality, you own your refusal, it is something you do not want to do for whatever reason. Explain your real reasons without looking for excuses or lying. Show empathy with the other person, you are refusing his or her request, but not him or her.

Let's take a look at the keys to do it correctly without looking bad to anyone.

Key 1. Avoid giving a blunt refusal, try to say something else. A resolute and solitary 'no' can generate discomfort, distance, resentment?

Key 2. Differentiate between the person and the request. Just because you reject a specific request does not mean that you reject the person who is asking for it. Make it clear.

Key 3. Offer alternatives. Saying "no, but I propose..." and giving other possibilities softens the refusal and makes the receiver feel understood. Sometimes by giving these alternatives we solve their problems much better than if we were to do it ourselves at that moment (simply because we may be in a hurry or stressed). Some examples of these alternatives could be:

"I can't today, but if you stop by first thing tomorrow morning we'll do it."

"I can't, but I know someone who could solve the problem for you."

"I don't have that information, but if you go to this website they will tell you everything."

Key 4. Empathize by giving an explanation that brings you closer to the other. *"I appreciate that you thought of me, the project seems very interesting to me, however, I like to dedicate my evenings to my family because...".*

Key 5. Pay attention to tone. Avoid using a hostile or harsh tone. Be polite and give the refusal in a firm but relaxed tone.

Key 6. Balance. The key to harmonious relationships (with ourselves and others) is balance.

Saying 'no' is not a bad thing, never saying it is.

In summary, reflect on the way of saying 'no' that best suits you and remember that the most important thing is:

1. Empathize: understand the request, know its purpose, its need.
2. Clearly state my objective: avoid excuses and justifications.
3. Offer alternatives.

I assure you that it is possible to say 'no' without damaging a personal relationship, sometimes even the alternatives you propose can have more satisfactory results for that person and above all for you. I hope it helps you!

DIFFICULT CONVERSATIONS: WHEN SOMEONE DOES NOT PERFORM

There are conversations that can be particularly difficult. When we have someone on our team who is not performing as well as we expect, we can lose patience, or even take drastic measures that we may later regret.

I am going to present one of the techniques that I had to use very few times but when I did it turned out to be very effective. It is a methodology to manage underperformance, that is, when someone in your team does not reach the results expected of him.

It is important that we help our employees to correct deviations in their performance before the consequences become irreversible.

It is important that we approach this conversation as something constructive, as an aid for our collaborator to achieve better results. In no case should it be approached as an accountability if we want it to be truly effective.

Before applying it, we must ensure that we have proposed clearly defined objectives following the SMART model (specific, measurable, achievable, relevant and time-bound) and that we have led our team in a way that facilitates the best possible performance. I explain this in detail in my book *Motivated Teams, Productive Teams*.

If, in spite of this, the results are not as expected, it is time to apply the following steps:

Step 1: Describe the situation. It is important to base this on facts and objective data, i.e. not to justify it with opinions or personal feelings. First of all, we explain what the expected performance was, according to the previously agreed objectives, and compare it with the results obtained. It is crucial that we can clearly and unequivocally show the gap between the current and desired situation.

Step 2: Explain the consequences and effects of these results. Make it very clear the reasons that make us highlight this situation to our collaborator, as well as the consequences they entail.

Step 3: Listen to what your employee has to say about the causes that led to this result. It is important to listen actively, on the one hand, this will make our collaborator see our interest in knowing their version, and on the other hand it will give us the opportunity to have more details of what may have gone wrong, their needs or other information that we may need to know and that may be relevant. In short, it will allow us to better understand the situation.

Step 4: Review of objectives. After listening to our collaborator, we may conclude that the objectives were too ambitious. In that case we could consider redefining those objectives to a more accessible level, especially to avoid the frustration that can be generated by having unattainable objectives. It is a matter of agreeing together on what would be appropriate and reasonable results.

Step 5: Offer and ask for alternatives to address the situation. To do this, we will ask a series of open-ended questions and encourage our partner to make suggestions for actions to help improve results.

Step 6: Action plan. Once the appropriate results and different alternatives have been reviewed, it is time to specify and agree on the actions to be taken to achieve them. What are you going to do? When? How? Where? In addition, the consequences of not complying with this agreement must be made clear.

Step 7: Follow-up. Finally, a date should be set to follow up on both the action plan and the results obtained.

Step 8: Appreciate the effort and maintain a cordial relationship with your collaborator.

I have not only tested this technique myself, but I have also guided numerous clients in applying it with their employees. The results have been very positive.

Giving them the opportunity to rectify before taking other more drastic measures can lead to mutual benefit. Knowing how to communicate this can make all the difference.

CONFLICT MANAGEMENT

A conflict does not have to be something negative if it is managed properly, it can even be a great opportunity to address issues that are often uncomfortable and solve them at the root.

What is really negative is to let a problem fester instead of dealing with it in a constructive way. When this happens, the atmosphere becomes rarefied, people become demotivated, they hold grudges, relationships break down, trust is undermined, and it's all negative consequences. It becomes a liability for any team. Therefore, it is not a matter of avoiding conflicts, but of managing them properly.

On the subject of conflict management, there are two habits that Stephen Covey pointed out in his book *The 7 Habits of Highly Effective People* that I think are fundamental to keep in mind.

- Fourth habit: Think win-win.
- Fifth habit: Seek first to understand and then to be understood.

Think win-win
When we go in with the mentality of winning at all costs, even when we have to raze the other party, we may win in the short

term, but in the medium or long term this can take a costly toll on us. It can backfire on us, especially because we can destroy a personal or professional relationship.

This win-win mentality means seeking mutual benefit, and helps powerfully to find balance in human relations with a sense of common good and fairness. This attitude enables the achievement of shared satisfactions among all those involved in a negotiation or conflict process. This model represents mutually satisfactory benefits, in addition to the fact that it involves reciprocal learning and mutual influence.

Seek first to understand and then to be understood
When we listen to someone sincerely we are achieving a double objective:

- On the one hand, we are collecting very valuable information that we must take into account when resolving the conflict, understanding the motives of the other, what has bothered him, what he expects from us. It is information that we need to collect in order to be able to resolve that conflict.

- On the other hand, and no less important, listening has a tremendously positive effect on the other person. If that person perceives that we care about his or her version and what he or she has to tell us, his or her level of aggressiveness or defensive attitude will decrease. The level of tension will relax and will facilitate the dialogue and, as a consequence, the probabilities of resolving the conflict in a satisfactory way.

Once this is done, once we have heard the other person's version, it will be our turn to speak. The fact that we have previously listened to our interlocutor will increase his receptiveness and the probability that he will also listen to what we have to say.

This is the habit that sustains the need to empathetically understand the other in order to be understood and to be able to build more constructive interpersonal relationships. The importance of empathic listening in the process of human communication stands out especially in this habit. Although all habits of effectiveness are closely related to emotional intelligence, this habit is to a greater degree because of its own emotional connotations.

The history of conflicts in all psychological and social fields reflects the absence of this understanding, first, and the unfortunate practice of negotiations, later.

Emotional intelligence plays a fundamental role in the conflict management process; being able to manage the torrent of emotions generated in a discussion is key to a positive and constructive outcome for both parties.

HOW TO MEDIATE OTHER PEOPLE'S CONFLICTS

When we lead a team, there will be times when we witness conflicts between members of our teams. Here our mission as a leader is to help them resolve them.

There is a technique that I have used on numerous occasions that is very effective in mediating third party disputes. It is the double iceberg technique.

First of all, it is essential to remain as neutral as possible. If we take one side or the other, we will never be able to help resolve it, but rather the opposite.

The first thing we have to do is to ask a fundamental question to both parties: Do you want to resolve this conflict? If the answer is yes, 50% of the work is already done.

Only on one occasion have I ever been answered 'no' to this question, and when they did I responded, "Are you serious that you want to spend eight hours a day working in this environment?". When this person reflected on my question, they finally recognized that it was best to work it out.

Another question the mediator should ask before getting involved in the resolution is, "Do you want me to help you resolve the conflict?" It is important that we are given permission to be part of the solution.

What does this methodology consist of?
Let's assume that two parties or persons are involved in the conflict: A and B.

The following is worked with each of the parties:

- Ask A:
  -Description of the complaint.
  -Make the list of facts: description of behaviors as objectively as possible.
  -Making the list of requests: this consists of writing "It would be great to work with B if...", i.e., listing what would have to happen for this to happen.
  -Make the list of concessions: what A would be willing to do to get B to do what is indicated in the list of requests.

- Ask B for the same as described above, from his/her position.
- Negotiate concessions, i.e., what each party is willing to do.
- Set a day to follow up and see progress.

Every time I have applied this methodology I have been surprised that the list of A requests and the list of B concessions coincide in approximately 70-80% (and vice versa).

So there is a very good basis to work that conflict. Taking that 70-80% and making an action plan to carry it out by both parties generates a reconciliatory attitude that is a great start to resolve that conflict.

It is essential to follow up a few days later. Ideally, after one or two weeks it is a good idea to sit down and see if both parties have fulfilled their commitment.

Keep in mind that if one day there is a complicated situation, a peak of stress or some unexpected event, the atmosphere may heat up and someone may skip what was agreed upon. This does not mean that the process has not worked, but it does require that both parties sit down again with their mediator to analyze what has happened and resume what has been agreed.

KEYS TO MANAGE YOUR BOSS

Managers should not forget that, in addition to managing their teams, they also have to manage their relationship with their boss. If the relationship with their superiors is good, it will be easier for them to get what they need for their teams. If, on the other hand, the relationship is not nurtured, it can be a source of additional stress and conflict. This is why it is worth paying attention to this issue.

Below, I want to share some guidelines for a healthy relationship with your boss. These points are based not only on my own experience, but also on the testimonials I hear when I work with my clients, both managers and their bosses.

Here are my tips for properly managing your relationship with your boss:

Focus on what really matters. If you have not been given clearly defined objectives, ask them to at least indicate the main priorities. There are times when energy and time are invested in doing very well tasks that do not bring results and that are totally secondary, thinking that maybe that is what is expected of them.

If you have a problem, propose solutions and not just complaints. A boss needs us to make his day-to-day life easier. If we really have a complaint with a serious problem that needs your intervention, let's make it a little easier by proposing alternatives to solve the situation.

Take responsibility for your mistakes and learn from them, do not try to hide them or blame others for your mistakes. If you make a habit of blaming others, sooner or later both your colleagues and your boss will realize it, and this will have its consequences, not only in your relationship with your boss, but also with the rest of the team.

Communicate in the same style as them, they may like us to give more or less details, or many or few figures. As a general rule, managers tend to prefer a brief, concise and to-the-point communication style, although there may be exceptions. Find out which style best connects with your boss.

Use your preferred means of communication, some people choose face-to-face, others however choose telephone or email. There may also be a medium that you find particularly annoying, such as WhatsApp or e-mail for some, in which case it should be avoided. Adapt to their preferences.

Proactivity. If you already have a certain degree of experience and know what you have to do, be proactive. Anticipate and take initiative, don't wait for instructions to take action. But make sure those actions are in line with what is expected of you.

Solve problems, make your boss's day-to-day life easier, let him/her see that you add value. Resolute people are usually highly valued.

Do not take criticism as something personal, but as something constructive, keep in mind that we cannot improve if we do not know where to put the focus. Accept criticism as an opportunity to improve your work. It would even be a good idea to ask for feedback in case you don't get any kind of signal. At least you will know if you are going in the right direction.

When stress levels are high, avoid being annoying with trivialities or increasing the level of tension even more. If you need to discuss an issue, wait until the time is right so that your boss is more receptive to what you have to say. You will get better results.

Be collaborative with your colleagues, someone who works well in a team is always better perceived. Offer to help your colleagues, but make sure that your tasks are covered, do not deviate from your objectives. You will earn not only the appreciation of your colleagues, but also that of your boss.

Adapt your way of communicating to the environment, perhaps you are a manager who has to communicate both with operators on the production line and with the steering committee. Communicating at the management level requires improving the ability to analyze, synthesize and have a global vision at the CEO level.

Prepare your speech before you speak, organize the information you may need so that you can present it in an orderly and efficient manner. Don't beat around the bush or ramble, they will get the feeling that you are wasting their time. Remember that bosses usually like you to be clear, concise and to the point.

Manage your time well, it is important to meet deadlines.

Bosses often have a high sense of urgency. When they use the expression "I need it as soon as possible" try to specify the date or even the time. Not everyone has the same sense of urgency, 'soon' can mean two hours or two days, depending on the person. Believe me, this creates a lot of misunderstandings and some conflict.

Show gratitude and recognition for their contributions. They, like anyone else, also need recognition.

Your boss is also flesh and blood, he/she has his/her problems, difficulties, insecurities and emotions, keep this in mind. There are times when they may have a high level of stress and need a large dose of emotional intelligence to avoid infecting their teams. Use your empathy, try to understand their point of view.

Character incompatibility. There are times when one strives to do things well, to have ideas, to be proactive, efficient, brief, etc... and then hits a wall time and time again. It is a very difficult and complex situation, especially when it does not happen to other less competent colleagues. It may be the case of character incompatibility. In these cases there are tools (self-awareness reports such as DISC or Belbin) that can help to identify these differences, analyze them in an aseptic way and make adaptations on both sides to facilitate day-to-day work. This, in fact, is something I often work on with my clients.

Ask for regular meetings, just to discuss your concerns with your team, both on a day-to-day and professional basis. Above all, share with them the actions you develop with the team, what you do and above all how you do it, in your day-to-day work with them. Ask for feedback *once* the meeting is over.

Provide suggestions agreed upon with other colleagues, propose to hold workshops to exchange ideas to improve as a company and that these requests or suggestions can be transferred hierarchically.

Some examples: I remember a case of a Director who told me about his Warehouse Manager, saying that he was a great guy, but that he spent his time polishing the warehouse. Specifically, he told me: "I don't need to have the warehouse in tip-top shape, what I need is for him to optimize the space so that I don't have to rent the warehouse next door, which costs me a lot of money". This Warehouse Manager, however, was not aware of this priority, and put all his energy into the wrong task. He was not focusing on what really mattered. So if the objectives are not clear, it is important to ask where to put the focus.

On another occasion, a director told me that one of the middle managers, although he was very good at his job and managed his team and their tasks very well, when it came to sitting on the steering committee he did not know how to communicate results or their needs. He focused on technicalities that the CEO could not understand. It was like speaking different languages. This director felt that this team leader needed to be able to have more capacity for analysis, synthesis and communication at the steering committee level. He needed a global vision and to prepare his speech before speaking. Not knowing how to express himself or sell himself affected his personal brand within the company and prevented him from transmitting his message correctly to management.

In conclusion, your boss can become your ally or your worst nightmare, these guidelines can give you an idea of what you can do and how you can anticipate to improve the relationship and perhaps avoid some headaches.

KEYS TO BUILDING TRUST

What is trust? Why is it important for a leader to build trust? What increases or decreases the level of trust we inspire? How can leaders build and maintain high levels of trust?

Stephen Covey talks about the "emotional bank account", where he explains the importance of building a positive balance in our relationship with the people around us. When the balance is positive in this "emotional bank account" we will gain the respect and trust of others.

> *For a leader, one of the easiest ways to build a positive balance of the "emotional bank account" is to build an environment of trust with his or her team.*

Next, let's take a look at the keys to building trust with our collaborators:

Key 1: Always tell the truth.
Being the leader means that co-workers act on your word, so make sure it's the truth. Nothing is more destructive to trust than finding out someone is lying to you.

Key 2: Keep your promises.
Being the leader, you have to deal with so many people and say things that, sometimes, are really hard to keep. Don't break your promises. If you say you're going to do something, make sure you do it.

Key 3: Practice active listening.
While talking to your employees, make sure you are fully attentive during the conversation and give them enough time to express their opinion. When conversing with them, put their needs first. When your employee feels listened to, the quality of that conversation improves tremendously, as does the leader-employee relationship.

Key 4: Always be fair to everyone.
Be consistent with office friends. While you're at work, make it clear that you treat everyone equally. If you treat some people better than others, it will soon result in a deficit in the "emotional bank account" and even generate unrest among members of your team.

Key 5: Lead by example.
There are bosses who set standards for their colleagues and subordinates, but do not follow their own rules. There is nothing more convincing than by example, if you yourself do what you ask your team to do, your request will be much more coherent and powerful.

Key 6: Help your team learn and grow.
Invest the time and resources necessary to train and coach your team. This will prepare them to perform their jobs better, work more productively and with greater confidence.

Key 7: Tackle problems constructively.
If there are problems related to the work of some of your collaborators, talk openly with them, tell them how you feel and what you expect them to do. The aim is to give constructive feedback and prevent the problem from escalating or recurring.

Key 8: Let them see that you trust them.
If you know your team is working well, offer them recognition and make it clear that you trust them. This will have a very motivating effect on your team.

In conclusion, without trust a team cannot function effectively. A good leader is a fundamental piece in the generation of trust within a team and it is essential that this exists so that there is cooperation between each of its members.

PERSONAL BRANDING

AND NETWORKING

The leader is the visible face of the team, in good times and bad. In addition, he/she must manage both internal and external communication.

When we are developing our professional career, moving to a new position, creating new ideas or projects, it is important to make ourselves known, make contacts, look for synergies, collaborations, possible clients, possible suppliers, in other words: take care of our network of contacts.

Personal relationships can not only provide us with the support we may need, but we can also find other points of view, new ideas, etc... That in our closest circle, but it is also convenient to widen our circle and take care of it.

WHAT DO WE HAVE TO DO TO TAKE CARE OF OUR NETWORK OF CONTACTS?

Add value. It is important to add value to our personal relationships. It is like an emotional bank, if we go to the ATM and all we do is withdraw bills but never deposit them, there will come a time when the ATM will not give us any more. Well, with the emotional bank it is similar, if we only ask and never give, the same thing will happen to us in the end.

Active listening. Active listening is a very important skill when it comes to cultivating personal relationships. When our interlocutor feels listened to, the quality of that conversation and that personal relationship improves enormously. And not only that..., there is an enormous amount of information that we miss out on by not actively listening. Information that can be relevant when it comes to achieving our goals.

Think win-win. When we talk about personal relationships it is also important to keep in mind the win-win attitude. Practicing win-win means looking for compromise solutions, where neither party loses out. If we go on a rampage, we may win in the short term, but over time it will take its toll.

Offline networking. Offline networking, i.e. face-to-face, consists of interacting with people in person, attending events that may be of interest such as conferences, networking sessions, trade shows, etc. You may not find a client or someone may not give you the job of your life, but this is like sowing seeds, the more you sow the more likely it is that some of them will germinate and bear fruit. There are times when great opportunities arise due to a chained succession of small actions that follow one after another, and in the end you come to the conclusion that none of those actions in isolation would have had any result; each and every one of them were necessary for a great opportunity to arise.

Online networking. It is also necessary to cultivate online networking, that is to say, social networks that, if well used, can be very useful when it comes to making yourself known and creating your personal brand. LinkedIn is increasingly used at a professional level. Having a well cared for and well updated profile on LinkedIn is the best business card you can have in these times. In addition, this is an extraordinary way to keep in touch with former colleagues. In my case, I spent ten years working in other countries, and thanks to social networks I have been able to keep in touch throughout this time with colleagues who have changed countries or companies. In some cases, I have even been able to keep in touch with university colleagues after years of not having heard from them.

Be grateful. Finally, I would like to dedicate a few lines to talk about gratitude. And the word 'thank you' is one of the words we forget to pronounce the most, and it is so necessary sometimes... There are studies that show how gratitude is a source of happiness, not only for the one who receives the gratitude, but even more for the one who offers it. I invite you to try it.

WHY IS IT IMPORTANT FOR A LEADER TO TAKE CARE OF HIS OR HER PERSONAL BRAND?

The leader is the visible face of the team, who must feel that his or her concerns and interests are being represented by the leader to the other work groups and external groups.

What is personal branding? It is the mark that our presence leaves on others, the impression we leave on others. A good personal brand gives credibility and inspires trust. Nowadays personal branding is not something exclusive to celebrities. Moreover, nowadays, with social networks, we have a great opportunity to cultivate our personal brand and what we project to others.

A good personal brand gives credibility and inspires trust.

It is also important to have integrity and consistency, we can not give a good professional image online if we are not really offline. When you publish something on the network you better be true and authentic, otherwise it is very easy for someone to give you away.

LINKEDIN, A GREAT ALLY FOR YOUR PERSONAL BRAND AND NETWORK OF CONTACTS

I firmly believe that nowadays every professional should be on LinkedIn and have a well maintained and updated profile. Even using it on a daily basis.

I started using LinkedIn in 2006, at that time my contacts in this network were exclusively work colleagues from Ireland, Holland or France, who were quite geographically mobile and the best way to keep in touch with each other was through this social network. We could change country, company, e-mail address or even phone number, and still this network allowed us to keep in touch. This allowed me to keep in touch with them when I returned to Spain, and today, despite the years that have passed and the fact that practically all of us have changed countries or companies, we are still in touch.

At the beginning, I only accepted invitations from people I knew personally, mainly in my professional environment, I spent several years with about fifty contacts. Later, when I launched my own company, I decided to expand my network of contacts more actively to have more visibility and work on my personal brand; today I have more than 8,500 contacts and my network is expanding day by day.

In addition, it helps me to add value with my publications, put in contact professionals looking for collaborations, get new clients, etc, etc.

It is like having an updated business card. Moreover, for those of us who have a short memory for retaining faces and names, it is a great ally. In fact, in recent years, when I meet people at my conferences and workshops, or at any other event, instead of exchanging cards, we connect on LinkedIn.

I once asked an acquaintance if he was on LinkedIn and he replied: "I'm not because I'm not looking for a job". This is a mistake. We must be very clear that it is not necessary to be looking for a job or clients to be on LinkedIn. While it is true that it also serves to find professional opportunities, it is a network that serves for much more.

If you are not yet on LinkedIn do not wait any longer to create your profile, it does not have to be perfect with all the details, in fact it is something that should be continuously updated.

During the first years, my profile had hardly any information, only my university studies and the most important positions in my professional career. Little by little I added more information, and I keep updating it frequently every time there is something new. If you are already on LinkedIn do not hesitate to look for my profile, I will be happy to add you to my network of contacts and exchange opinions about this book.

WHAT GOOD IS IT FOR A LEADER TO BE ON LINKEDIN?

Precisely this network can be a great ally for the personal brand and network of contacts of any leader, even if he or she is not the owner of the company.

These are, among others, the uses we can give it as leaders:

- To give visibility to our company as well as to the products or services it offers.
- To give visibility to the achievements of our team and our company.
- Work on our personal brand with *posts* and publications that reflect our values and with which we can inspire others.
- Generate trust and credibility, if you take care that what you publish is authentic.
- Give recognition, both to your team and to other professionals.
- Receive recognition or testimonials of your professional career, again a good ingredient for your personal brand.
- Keep in touch with peers and other professionals and keep up to date with their careers (the world goes round and round, believe me...).
- Curriculum is constantly updated.
- An excellent alternative to your business card, plus you can carry it on your cell phone and always have it at hand.
- A good showcase to recruit new candidates for your team.
- Find customers and/or suppliers.

If you are an entrepreneur, freelancer or business owner, both you and your company should be on LinkedIn.

As an example, I would like to mention Rafael Juan, CEO of Vicky Foods, whom I have been following for some time now and who makes excellent use of LinkedIn and other social media such as Twitter and Instagram. He gives visibility to every achievement of his company and his team, does not skimp on offering recognition left and right and really inspires a healthy and motivational leadership in everything he publishes. He has undoubtedly achieved an impeccable personal brand.

In conclusion, our personal brand and our network of contacts are great resources when it comes to progress professionally and achieve our goals. LinkedIn can be a great ally if you use it well. Taking care of all this is essential, it is like a plant that needs to be watered so that it continues to grow strong and give us its fruits.

And you, how do you take care of your network?

PART 3:

THE LEADER'S PRODUCTIVITY

- THE NEW PRIORITIES OF A LEADER
- KEYS TO SETTING SUCCESSFUL GOALS
- TIME QUADRANTS
- PARETO PRINCIPLE
- GTD METHODOLOGY
- PROCRASTINATION
- EFFECTIVE MEETINGS, MEETINGS WITH ACTION
- PRODUCTIVITY OR PRESENTEEISM?

THE NEW PRIORITIES OF A LEADER

One of the issues that my clients with teams need to work on the most is time management. Has it ever happened to you that you have been doing things all day long and in the end you haven't achieved anything? Busy all day long, but without reaching your goals and also totally exhausted.

Clearly, if we want to achieve our objectives and execute a good action plan, we have to get down to work, we have to do things. However, we have to clearly establish our priorities if we want to invest our time in what will lead us to the results we are looking for or that are expected of us.

WHY DO YOU LACK TIME?

It is very common for someone with a team to feel overwhelmed by the lack of time. There are several factors that contribute to this:

Managing a team is a very complex task that requires additional time and energy: assigning tasks, following up, giving instructions, training them, communicating, listening, etc...

Continuous interruptions. When you lead a team, it is common for them to come to your office either to solve a question, bring you a report or ask you for a vacation or a salary increase. They demand your attention, your energy and your time.

Lack of delegation. Many times the fact that you know how to do a task makes you fall into the trap of doing it yourself instead of delegating it. Now you manage a team, your mission is to get your team to do those tasks. That will require an initial investment of time, but if you choose the right tasks to delegate and the right person, you will get a return on that investment.

Letting ourselves be kidnapped by the urgent, ignoring the important. This happens very often, these interruptions, these urgencies distract us and do not make us focus on the short term, we go putting out fires and in the end we lose the north. This makes us not to be productive and in the end we do not achieve the results that really matter.

The new responsibilities acquired when a professional is promoted. Often their hierarchical position puts them in charge of new responsibilities, including leading a team; it is crucial to be aware that the way they prioritize their tasks will change.

Not knowing how to prioritize or optimize where to invest our time and effort. This is often a consequence of the previous point. As we have new responsibilities, sometimes it is difficult to prioritize them, and therefore to assess when and how to manage each task.

On the one hand, managing a team of you means that there will be activities that no longer correspond to you directly, but will have to be done by your team and you will be responsible for their correct execution. This means that we have to rely on our team to optimize our productivity and distinguish which tasks we should focus on.

I HAVE A DILEMMA: MY TEAM OR MY TASKS?

Many of my clients who lead a team for the first time often have this dilemma: Do I focus on taking care of my team or on executing the tasks that need to be done? This is often the case for very good professionals who, as a reward for their work and professional merits, have been promoted and now manage a team.

This is often the case, but the fact that they are very good professionals does not mean that they find it easy to manage people. Leading teams is a delicate and complicated task, in fact, it is a great challenge even for those who have experience managing people.

These professionals go from being experts in what they used to do, to not knowing how to perform their new position, simply because they have not assimilated their transformation from task manager to people manager.

They tend to act by doing what they do best, i.e., executing tasks. So they focus on habits and behaviors that have brought them success in previous experiences, because they think that's how they can solve the situation.

What is the result of all this?
What these professionals tend to do is to return to their comfort zone, i.e., instead of assuming their new role as

team leader, they focus on the tasks. They do this mainly to "save time", avoid confrontations, or think that they know how to do it better,... That is why it is so difficult for them to delegate.

Let's remember that they are usually great professionals, experts in those tasks and very committed to their work, so they tend to assume the functions of their team executing those tasks.

> *As a consequence, their day-to-day work becomes a hell full of stress, lack of time, excessive workload.*

Here the key is to distinguish which tasks can't be done by anyone else but us and which tasks, even if we know how to do them very well (even better than our team) we have to delegate. We must make those delegable tasks to be executed through our team

It is clear that at the beginning we will need to invest time in training someone to do those activities, but once that training is finished we will have developed our team and we will have more time to do what we really need to do.

In summary, what we would have to do is:

- Identify tasks that only we can carry out and make them our priority.
- Identify those tasks that our team can do and train them to do them autonomously.

TURNING THE STRATEGIC PLAN INTO ACTIONS

The company's strategic plan will set our priorities, i.e. what is really important, when it comes to managing our time. Therefore, all our actions and those of our team must go in the right direction, in line with the company's objectives and strategies. We will be key players in ensuring that the message reaches from the top to the last link in the chain and that these strategies are translated into concrete actions so that the company achieves the performance and productivity necessary to comply with the strategic plan.

Some time ago in one of my workshops I asked the question: "Do you have clearly defined objectives? In the room were the management team, some with a slight and timid shake of the head said that they were not so clear. The CEO, who was there, reacted with surprise and anger, since just the week before they had presented the strategic plan with a resounding event.

We must realize that these strategic plans, which are the pillars that support where the company wants to go, must be "translated" into concrete actions. This is precisely where many companies stumble.

It would not be the first time that a CEO gets irritated with his team because they don't seem to know what they have to do. Sometimes we think that by defining the strategic plan everyone is clear about what is expected of them. But this is not the case.

The strategic plan is made at such a high level that it can be very abstract for the last link in the chain.

A warehouse forklift operator may see the strategic plan and not bat an eyelid because he does not know what his contribution can be to something that is so far away from him. For this "translation" it is essential to involve middle management from the beginning to ensure that they understand and internalize the company's mission, vision and values at the highest level, and that they in turn transmit it to their teams in a language that is "understandable" to everyone, i.e., concretizing it in the actions that must be carried out in the different areas to achieve these goals.

Occasionally, a director would tell me how his middle management were focused on the details of the operations and were not able to have the perspective to have a more global view of the company's situation.

The manager has to be able to adapt his language in order to understand and be understood, both by his superiors in management committees and strategic meetings, as well as by workers who in some cases do not even have a primary school education. Therefore, their role is fundamental in any company and it is not an easy one. Therefore, the development, education and training of middle managers in this field should not be underestimated.

How to do it?

Middle managers are the key players in converting this strategy into concrete tasks with a good action plan. This action plan must be well defined, identifying not only what is going to be done, but also when, how, where and by whom. And of course, every action plan needs to be followed up to ensure that progress is made or redefined when the occasion demands.

Middle managers are key players in "translating" this strategic plan into concrete objectives and actions for their teams.

It is important to work at the level of management teams and middle management of the company to develop a healthy and motivating leadership, training them in practical tools that help tremendously in the management of their teams.

It often happens that the message is diluted as it "goes down a level". If we have very hierarchical structures, we run this risk. When the message is shared and transversal, that is to say, in cooperation and not in competition, everyone will become a carrier, an agent of change.

In my *High Performance Team Development* workshops I guide companies and their leaders in defining objectives together and help them create the necessary action plans to achieve those goals together with their collaborators. This is developed in workshops, where everyone participates actively and dynamically, facilitating the work of landing that strategic plan, sometimes so abstract, in concrete actions that everyone understands.

Involving employees in this process tremendously increases their understanding of the strategic plan. The effect on the bottom line is enormous.

KEYS TO SETTING SUCCESSFUL GOALS

Setting goals and achieving them has a very powerful motivational effect. And not only that, it also has a "snowball" effect, if you achieve your goal you will get energy and motivation to go for the next one.

Let's take a look at the main keys to do it in the most effective way:

Key 1: Set yourself short, medium and long term goals. In fact, we should aim to have at least one goal for each of our days. If we complete our day achieving those goals, we will feel much more satisfied with ourselves, with our life, more fulfilled and happier. Try to set daily, weekly and monthly goals.

Key 2: Visualize your goal in detail. In this way we are programming our "radar" to help us capture all that information that is relevant to achieve our goals. Has it ever happened to you that you have bought a certain brand of car and suddenly you see it everywhere? That is simply because if we put the focus on something, we will be much more alert to capture all the information related to everything that brings us closer to what we want to achieve.

Key 3: Write down your objectives. Writing down your objectives also helps, to order ideas, to internalize them. It is said that when a goal is written down, it is 80% more likely to be achieved.

Key 4: Specific. You have to be as specific as possible about what you want, in as much detail as possible. It's like when you go on a trip and program your GPS: the more details you give about your destination, the better it will show you the way.

Key 5: Measurable. You need to be able to measure your goal, to quantify your progress, to see how far you are from getting there and to monitor whether you are going in the right direction. Seeing your progress will help you stay motivated.

Key 6: Achievable. If you set a goal that is far beyond your means, not only do you run the risk of not achieving it, but you will have a high probability of becoming frustrated. It is a matter of measuring your strengths and setting realistic goals. It can also happen that a goal may at first seem totally out of your reach, what I call an "elephant goal", but how would you eat an elephant? Slice by slice, right? Well, that's what you have to do with your goal, divide it into sub-goals, so that when you eat the first slice you get energy and motivation to get on to the next one and so on, until you eat the whole elephant.

Key 7: Relevant. If a goal is too easy you are not going to get that motivating effect I was talking about at the beginning. The harder it is to achieve a goal, the more motivating it will be to achieve it. The ideal is to have a good balance between achievable and challenging.

Key 8: The time factor. An objective or a project that does not have a delivery date runs the risk of being infinitely dilated in time, so infinitely, that it may never be fulfilled. That is why it is crucial to set a date for our objectives.

Key 9: Ecological. Just because a target is "ecological" doesn't mean it won't harm the environment. It has nothing to do with it. It means that it doesn't conflict with your values, or with some other goal, or that it doesn't harm anyone who is important to you. If it's not ecological, when you achieve it, it won't make you happy.

Key 10: Reward. Finally, every objective must have its reward. Why do you want to achieve this objective? What is the purpose? What will it mean for you to achieve it? That "what for?" is going to be our driving force in the weak moments, in the days when we lack the strength to continue. If we have a purpose, a compelling reason, something that is the reward for achieving our goal, it will be much easier to stay motivated.

All these are the ingredients that every good objective must meet in order to be formulated correctly. Have you already set your objectives?

TIME QUADRANTS

Where to start? Well, that's what it's all about, learning to better manage our priorities and our time to achieve our goals. To do this, in my workshops on time management, one of the first concepts I show is Stephen Covey's "time quadrants", who said that any task can be classified according to its importance and urgency.

Do you know the difference between 'urgent' and 'important'? A lot of people confuse it, I myself a few years ago didn't really know what the difference was, I even thought they were the same thing. But it's not.

What is **urgent** is something that cannot wait, that has to be done in the immediate term, for example, a house that is on fire, something that requires action at that very moment (regardless of its importance). To know if it is urgent, we simply have to ask ourselves "does this have to be done now?" (regardless of its importance or who does it, it may not be essential for you to do it). If the answer is 'yes', that task is urgent.

What **is important** is determined by our objectives, by what brings us closer to our goals, to what we want to achieve in our lives or in our jobs. For this it is essential that we have previously defined our objectives in the short, medium and long term. Once we have done this, when faced with a task we will ask ourselves "Does doing this bring me closer to my objectives?" If the answer is yes, then the task is important.

For example, for you as a leader:

- Anything that helps you achieve your company's strategic plan is important.
- Those tasks that only you can take care of and that you cannot delegate to anyone else would also fall into this category.

Based on these two criteria, Covey classified tasks into four quadrants:

Quadrant 1: Urgent and important.
That which cannot wait and which is also crucial for you. It is the quadrant of crises (an important client with a complaint, a project that is overdue, a fire in your house...). Any task in this quadrant has to be done by you and you have to do it now. The result of this quadrant dominating your life is stress, anxiety, burnout. No human body can stand it for long.

Quadrant 2: Important and not urgent.
It is that which can wait, but you must not give it up if you want to prosper. It is the leadership quadrant. The quadrant of personal development, planning, anticipation, proactivity, problem prevention, training, taking care of yourself, etc.

The result of working in this quadrant is success.

What do you have to do with this quadrant? Set it aside in your agenda, put a date on it, you don't have to do it right now, but make sure you don't leave it. In fact, we may have tasks that are currently in quadrant 2 and if we do not act, they may become quadrant 1 tasks. Imagine that you do not spend time taking care of yourself, and over time health problems arise, which eventually become urgent and important (illness, hospitalization, etc.).

Quadrant 3: Urgent and not important.
Although it may be important to others, but not to you. It can also be called the "illusion or mirage" quadrant. Why? Because it keeps you busy all day doing numerous tasks, you create the illusion that you have done a lot, but at the end of the day you have not achieved your goals.

What is the result of your day-to-day life being filled with this quadrant? Focusing on the short term and losing focus, losing perspective of where you really want to go.

What to do? You have to delegate this quadrant or learn to say 'no'. In fact, many are those who have problems with this quadrant: they let themselves be hijacked by the urgent, or they take care of other people's priorities instead of taking care of their own, or they find it hard to delegate tasks that are not crucial but steal their precious time.

Quadrant 4: Not important and not urgent.
The most absolute waste of time we can have. For example, we decide to take a well-deserved half-hour break in front of the television, which in the end turns into hours of trash TV. Or maybe we start looking on the Internet for what we need for a particular topic and in the end we are assaulted by the

remarketing of the day (those ads that chase you until you get caught) and you deviate from what you wanted to do, and without realizing you have spent hours surfing the net.

What is the result of your life being flooded with this quadrant? Total failure. The less time you waste in this quadrant, the better.

Quadrant 2 is the key: The more time we spend in this quadrant, the more we will reduce our quadrant 1, and the more we will take control of our life.

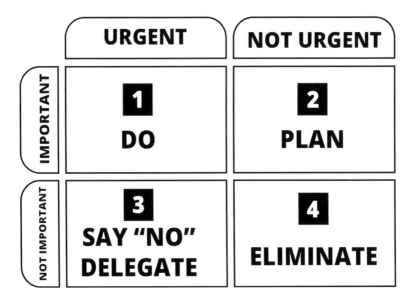

Conclusion: It is true that there may be part of the tasks in quadrant 1 that we cannot avoid, but a large part can be eliminated. How? By working on our quadrant 2 (planning, preventing, training, anticipating, taking care of ourselves...). And where can we get time for quadrant 2? Well, precisely from quadrants 3 and 4, that is: delegating, learning to say 'no', with more discipline and willpower. Keeping these principles in mind when choosing our priorities is the basis for good time management, so that we can successfully achieve our goals.

Both in my time management workshops and in *Leadership Development* processes with my clients (individually or in teams) I include more tools and information on how to better manage our time and priorities, but in my opinion (and from my own experience) the concept of time quadrants is a fundamental basis that, if well understood and applied, leads to excellent results.

Do you dare to apply it in your daily life?

PARETO PRINCIPLE

During my time as a student I remember that every time I had to prepare for an exam I would focus more on those topics or sections that were more likely to come out according to previous years' tests.

I would study the entire syllabus, although I would prepare especially well for those questions. That worked for me year after year. Without knowing it, I was applying the Pareto principle, which basically tells us to put more focus on what will give us the best results.

Look for that 20% of your tasks that generates 80% of your results!

This can even be applied to language learning. If we focus on the 20% of vocabulary, verbs, grammatical rules, etc. that are used 80% of the time, with much less effort we will achieve an acceptable level of that language.

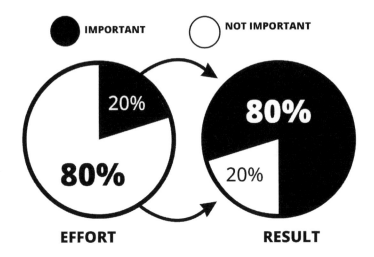

IMPORTANT NOT IMPORTANT

20%

80%

80%

20%

EFFORT RESULT

The principle is named after Vilfredo Pareto, an Italian economist who observed that 80% of wealth was owned by 20% of Italians, and has underpinned much of microeconomic thinking.

The business world as a whole seems to be consistent with the 80/20 principle, but its breakdown might be slightly different depending on each situation. These percentages can vary: 80/20, 75/25 or even 90/10. What really matters is understanding that a small percentage of your activities/causes (20%) are responsible for most of your results/effects (80%).

APPLICATION OF THE 80/20 PRINCIPLE IN THE COMPANY

Pareto theory is also very useful in business and organizational planning. The Pareto 80/20 rule is commonly used in many aspects of organizational and business management.

- 80% of the company's profit comes from 20% of its customers.
- 80% of the stock is made up of 20% of the references.
- 80% of the orders are concentrated in 20% of the references.

It is useful in specialized quality management, such as Six Sigma, planning, decision making and general performance management.

One of the applications of this principle in my time as Supply Chain Operations Manager was in warehouse inventories, making a cyclic count of all references. Those items that accounted for 80% of sales, those that rotated the most (20% of the items) were counted several times a year, while those that had hardly any movement (80% of the items) were counted only once a year. In this way, Stock Controllers could optimize inventory accuracy and their workload in the warehouse by focusing on what was really relevant.

With one of my clients who wanted to reduce the workload of the complaints management department, we also used this principle, analyzing and focusing on 20% of the causes or problems that generated 80% of customer complaints. This made it much more efficient to tackle the situation, reduce the risk of complaints and optimize the department's resources.

Pareto in project management

Pareto theory is also very useful in project management. How? For example:

If we take ten weeks to develop a project, and in only two weeks we can develop 80% of the functionality. It would take us eight weeks to develop the less crucial, but perhaps more difficult and complex 20%. In two weeks we could deliver a much faster turnaround of a viable product. The customer could even remove some less necessary, time-consuming and costly functionality.

PARETO IN TIME MANAGEMENT

The Pareto principle is extremely useful for bringing quick and easy clarity to complex situations and problems, especially when deciding where to focus effort and resources.

This same principle can be applied to your daily routine.

- 20% of your effort can generate 80% of the results.
- 80% of productivity loss is due to 20% of the causes.

Therefore, look for that 20% of your tasks that generate 80% of your results with three steps:

1. Clearly identify your objectives and activities that are key to your results, i.e. what is really important.
2. Apply the Pareto principle to prioritize your tasks.
3. Be sure to protect these key activities so that there are no deviations.

The objective here is:

- Those activities that provide you with the most relevant results and bring you closer to your objectives should form your to-do list.
- Those activities that rob you of time, detract from your productivity or even have a negative impact should be on your "don't do" list.
- What this means is that you must identify which tasks can be delegated, automated or eliminated altogether.

GTD METHODOLOGY

Getting Things Done or GTD is a productivity system created by David Allen, recognized worldwide as one of the most efficient methodologies for personal organization and that increases productivity while reducing stress and anxiety levels.

GTD is based on the principle that a person needs to free his mind from pending tasks by keeping them in a specific place, so that it is not necessary to remember what needs to be done and he can concentrate on accomplishing the tasks.

GTD in practice is applied in five steps:

Step 1 - Collect
It is the first step and consists of capturing 100% of all your pending issues, projects and tasks that you want or have to take care of.

You download all that stuff from your head and store it in your "inboxes", which can be emails, mobile apps, recorders, notepads, diaries, boards with sticky notes, etc.

Nowadays there are very sophisticated applications and software to manage tasks. In reality, it is not the tool but the use you make of the tool that really matters. A simple pen and paper can be very efficient if used well.

Step 2 - Clarifying

It consists of deciding what to do with each of the items you have collected in your inboxes. Possible scenarios:

A. No action is required. There are three possibilities here:

- **Discard** it completely.
- **Incubate** them or save them for later.
- **Archive** them as reference information.

B. It does require action. Then it will become a task and we will have different types:

- **Project**. If the task is complex, we classify it as a project and break it down into subtasks that we will manage in due time.
- **If it can be done in less than two minutes**, the action is executed at that moment. By doing this, the brain perceives that we are moving forward and we will be able to decrease the feeling of anxiety and stress that overwhelms many people when they feel stuck.
- **If it takes more than two minutes, we can opt for:**
  - **Delegating:** This occurs in those cases in which a task must be referred to another person to execute it. We will place the task in the "waiting list".
  - **Schedule**: Those tasks that need to be done on a specific date are reserved in our calendar or agenda.
  - **Defer:** Means to put that task on the "*to do list*".

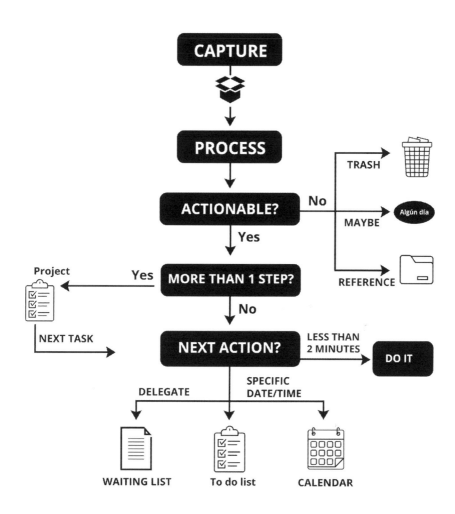

Step 3 - Organize

GTD recommends saving and organizing activities in lists. This way a person can fully dedicate himself to the execution of a task and free his mind without forgetting the rest of the pending tasks that we will keep registered in these lists. We can also manage to-do lists with applications such as Evernote, Trello, Google+ Lists or Google Calendar. Although it is not necessary a great technology, with pencil, paper and a calendar will be enough.

These are the lists suggested by the method:

- **To do list.** Having broken down the more complex actions or projects you have to do into simpler tasks, this list is where you will write down each of the next steps you have to do.
- **Projects.** Allen points out that any task that requires more than one action or step is itself a project, which you have to write down in this list to be reviewed periodically and transfer to the *"to do list"* the task or action that progresses the accomplishment of each project.
- **On hold.** This is the place for all the things that you have delegated or that a third party has to send you to continue the completion of a task or project.
- **Someday.** Here goes everything you'd like to do at some point, but it's not a priority.

Step 4 - Review

The lists that have been created should be reviewed periodically to decide what to do at any given time and to maintain control and reliability of our system.

Daily review: we will review our *"to do list"* and our agenda or calendar.

Weekly review: calendar, our tracking file, our project list, someday/maybe, etc.

General review: from time to time, we will check that we are still aligned with our objectives and vision and that we are moving in the right direction.

Step 5 - Doing

At this stage you have to do the tasks and actions that are on your list at the time and with the tools you have at your disposal.

This is just a brief summary of GTD, in David Allen's book and on the internet you can find very good resources and additional information.

Conclusion

The objective of all this is to create a work routine to get all your worries, ideas, tasks, thoughts, etc., out of your head and turn them into actions under control. This simple gesture helps tremendously for two reasons:

- **It reduces the stress level.** Having something in the back of your mind so that you don't forget it stresses you out, and this method avoids it.
- **Increases productivity.** GTD is a controlled system that ensures that our tasks are not forgotten and are executed.

In conclusion, a system to have the peace of mind that your tasks are under control.

PROCRASTINATION

Have you ever left something for later because at that moment you didn't know where to start? Or have you thought that, since you don't have time to do it perfectly now, you'd better leave it for later? Does this sound familiar? Well, these are symptoms of procrastination.

Procrastinating consists of delaying activities or situations that should be attended to, substituting them for other more irrelevant or pleasant situations.

This is something we have all experienced at one time or another.

What are the causes?

This can have different causes, these are some of the most frequent:

- Blocked by something that can stress us so much that we can become paralyzed.
- Fear of failure (or success).
- Indecision when we have to choose between several options.

- Not knowing how to do it.
- Perfectionism, until we have the perfect conditions to make it perfect we will not do it.
- Objectives that are too ambitious, so much so that they overwhelm.
- Trusting that there will be time to do it later.

How to overcome it?

Depending on the cause that originates this procrastination, we can take measures to overcome it, for example:

- Change the "I have to do it" to "I want to do it", this takes a lot of pressure off in case of blockage or fear of failure.
- Inform and train ourselves, in case we do not know how to do it.
- Without perfectionism, the perfect is the enemy of the good.
- Slicing the elephant. When the task is too large we will break it down into more accessible subtasks.
- Ten-minute rule. We are going to propose to dedicate at least ten minutes to the task, the great majority of the times we will continue more time since what it costs is to begin.
- Think of the reward, the relief we will feel when we take that task off our *to do list*.
- Share it with others. When we commit in front of others to do something, we are much more likely to do it because of public pressure.

If I had to recommend just one of these possible solutions, I would go with the ten-minute rule. It's actually a self-deception, but it works with spectacular results. I invite you to try it the next time you have trouble starting a task.

EFFECTIVE MEETINGS, MEETINGS WITH ACTION

After ten years working in Ireland and Holland, when I returned to Spain I had to get used to a very different work culture. Well, one of the biggest differences I found was the management of meetings. I realized that most of them started late, many were unprepared, everyone spoke at the same time, and what is worse, in the end little was learned.

In my time management workshops, many point out that one of the biggest "time thieves" are meetings. But how can we make a meeting really effective?

What I am about to tell you is no more and no less than what I used to do when I worked in Ireland and the Netherlands, and it was very productive.

Below, I describe the steps to take into account when convening a meeting, and it really makes the difference for it to be productive and a good investment of our time.

STEP 1: PLANNING

The first step is to consider whether or not this meeting is really necessary. Could it be solved with a phone call or an email? Or maybe just by talking to the main actor?

Above all, avoid unnecessary meetings.

If we finally come to the conclusion that the best way to resolve the issue is to bring the key people together, we should be very clear about the answers to the following questions:

- **Purpose:** What would the meeting be for?
- **Agenda:** What topics will be discussed?
- **Participants:** Who will attend? It is necessary to make sure that no one is absent or overbooked, otherwise the meeting will lose effectiveness.
- **Information:** What information is needed? Prepare a report, read some mail, collect some data, etc.

STEP 2: BEFORE THE MEETING

Once all the above questions have been answered, the meeting must be convened.

It is essential to communicate the details of the meeting to the stakeholders sufficiently in advance so that they can schedule it and organize to attend. To this end, it is important to:

Communicate to all stakeholders: date, time, place, agenda, duration and attendees.

Each and every one of the attendees should attend the meeting with their "homework done", i.e., prepare everything that may be needed for the meeting: reports, reading previous information, etc.

Here is an example of an e-mail meeting request:

Subject: **Meeting Invitation**

Dear Team,

We hope this message finds you well. We would like to invite you to an upcoming team meeting to discuss important matters and align our efforts. Please find the details below:

Attendees:
- John Smith (Team Lead)
- Jane Johnson (Marketing)
- Michael Williams (Finance)
- Sarah Davis (HR)
- Robert Miller (Design)
- Emily Wilson (Sales)

Date: September 5, 2023
Time: 2:00 PM (EST)
Location: Conference Room B

Total Duration: 1 hour

Agenda:
1. Opening remarks and welcome (5 minutes)
2. Project status update: goals and progress (15 minutes)
3. New marketing campaign proposal (20 minutes)
4. Employee feedback and engagement initiatives (10 minutes)
5. Team-building event planning (10 minutes)

Please come prepared with the information needed to discuss the agenda items and share your valuable insights. We look forward to a productive meeting.

STEP 3: DURING THE MEETING

It's time for the meeting. Let's see what are the keys to make it a success:

Moderator. It is convenient that someone acts as moderator of the meeting, it can be the organizer or any other person. This person will be in charge of making sure that all the points that follow are respected, that there is no rambling, that time is managed, that turns to speak are respected, that notes are taken and that the minutes of the meeting are taken.

Start on time. This is one of the unfinished business in Spain. And it is all a question of habits and company culture. If a company's employees get used to meetings starting a quarter of an hour late, they will always be late. However, if meetings start on time and they are met with a closed door, they are more likely to improve their punctuality in the end. It's just a matter of starting to do it.

Focus on the agenda. Socializing is all well and good, but we'd better leave it for the coffee machine. It's about covering all the agenda items one by one, avoiding digressions with typical conversations about soccer, politics, etc.

When there is a clear meeting agenda, it is much easier to stick to it.

Stick to the schedule. Have you ever been stuck in a meeting that you know when it starts, but you don't know when it ends? For this not to happen it is very important to respect the previous point, it helps to see how much of the agenda is left to cover in the time available. If we are running out of time, the agenda and the moderator will help us to get to the point.

Speaking time. This is probably one of the biggest differences between meetings in Spain and those in other Nordic countries. It is common for everyone to speak at the same time, to be interrupted or to form huddles and stop listening to the speaker. So it is important that this point is respected for the meeting to be productive.

Action plan. For the meeting to be useful, it is important to be clear about what comes next, i.e., what to do, who should do it, when and how. A good action plan should be the outcome of any effective meeting.

STEP 4: AFTER THE MEETING

To put the finishing touches on the meeting and to ensure that it is not just a bunch of good ideas and intentions, it is important to do the following after the meeting:

Written minutes: This is the best way to concretize and make sure that everyone is clear on the conclusions and actions of that meeting, even those who were unable to attend! The key information should be summarized: attendees, discussion, action plan, date of the next meeting...

This summary of the meeting does not have to be a long document, the idea is that the minutes should be something simple and practical and not another time thief (neither for the one who writes them nor for the one who has to read them).

Here is an example of a report that I used to send. As you can see, it is not necessary to invest a lot of time for the minutes to do their job. Simply forwarding the call mail and updating the information of who has or has not attended, main actions and how the follow-up is going to be done is enough.

Meeting Minutes and Action Plan

Date: September 5, 2023
Time: 2:00 PM - 3:00 PM
Location: Conference Room B

Present: Absent:
- John Smith (Team Lead)   - Emily Wilson (Sales)
- Jane Johnson (Marketing)
- Michael Williams (Finance)
- Sarah Davis (HR)
- Robert Miller (Design)

Agenda:
1. Opening remarks and welcome
2. Project status update: goals and progress
   Action Item: Each team member will provide an update on their respective project before the end of the month.
3. New marketing campaign proposal
   Action Plan: Jane to refine the proposal based on feedback and share with the team by Friday.
4. Employee feedback and engagement initiatives
   Action Plan: Sarah to create a detailed plan for engagement initiatives and circulate for review by next Wednesday.
5. Team-building event planning
   Action Plan: Robert to research and gather more information about the proposed team-building activities and present a finalized plan in the next meeting.

Next Meeting:
Date: October 2, 2023
Time: 2:00 PM - 3:00 PM
Location: Conference Room

Obviously this is something adaptable, a weekly operational meeting is not the same as a meeting to negotiate the contract of sale of a company.

Follow-up: we must follow up that the action plan is being carried out. Ideally, each individual should be responsible for informing the others when their action has been completed.

All these steps should be flexible and adjusted to each of the situations and different types of meetings.

In addition, we must choose the type of meeting that best suits our needs, from Japanese-style meetings, which are held standing up and last ten minutes, to meetings that can even last several days. Both the frequency and format should be optimized so that they are productive and do their job.

It's all pretty simple and really, it's common sense, but well applied it makes the difference between a meeting being a waste of time or something really productive.

What would you change from your last meeting? What will your next meeting be like?

PRODUCTIVITY OR PRESENTEEISM?

I remember when I started working in Ireland, I loved my job and I also wanted to make a good impression, so I stayed in the office for long hours.

Until one day, one of my colleagues warned me to stop doing it. He told me that, in the Nordic countries, if you work longer hours, you give the impression that you are not able to do your work in eight hours. You basically give the image of being an unproductive person. That surprised me a lot, since in Spain, spending long hours in the office was well regarded.

After ten years living and working outside Spain, I realized that in our country not only is presenteeism encouraged, but it can be confused with productivity. As a result, despite the fact that more hours are spent at work, more is not produced.

A few days ago an employer complained that one of his employees always arrived and left on time. He never stayed longer than the official schedule. This in principle should not be the criterion for evaluating performance, we would have to base it on the results achieved by that person.

We can have people on our team who keep their schedule to the letter and perform, and the opposite, people who spend more hours than anyone else in the office and fail to meet their objectives.

What is the result of encouraging presenteeism?

If we evaluate our employees by the amount of time they spend in the office, without setting clearly defined objectives, we run the risk of them spending hours and hours at their jobs that need not be productive. Moreover, it has been proven that after a certain number of hours we are no longer productive, not to mention the imbalances that arise between family life and professional life.

Long hours in the office that do not necessarily translate into productivity, but rather into:

- Cost of overtime
- Lack of family reconciliation
- Lack of motivation
- Lower productivity
- Fatigue
- Boredom

Do we penalize productivity?

How do we sometimes penalize productivity? When someone leaves early because they have finished their work, they can be saddled with more work until we "burn them out."

This also happens at the team level, when they perceive that the result of performing better may not be recognition, but the threat that maybe there are too many people and someone needs to be let go.

All this can make our team perceive that being productive can be counterproductive, that is, something that can have negative consequences. A paradox that I have seen on more than one occasion.

What options do we have?
I think there is a lot of work to be done in this direction, and that the solution lies in two keys:

- Clearly define the objectives and results to be achieved.
- Encourage self-responsibility and commitment within our teams.

It is clear that there are certain positions that require presence, such as those that offer a service to the public or establishments with business hours. But not all positions require that presence.

I am in favor of working by objectives, defining them clearly and basing our evaluation of the performance of our team members on the achievement of those objectives. If they choose to do so productively, the reward could be that they can leave the office early.

Let's set goals and let them choose how to organize themselves to achieve them.

This way we will get more motivation and commitment than if they simply interpret their work as spending hours sitting in the office.

To begin to put it into practice, certain steps must be taken:

- Define objectives clearly.
- Flexibility of schedules.
- Follow up on results.
- Reward productivity.
- Encourage commitment and self-responsibility.
- Good communication.

In summary, the number of hours spent in the office does not necessarily translate into productivity, let's set clear objectives and encourage commitment and self-responsibility. Let's base our performance and that of our teams on the results achieved.

PART 4:

TEAM LEADERSHIP

- HIGH-PERFORMANCE TEAM
- KEYS TO OPTIMIZE YOUR LEADERSHIP STYLE
- MOTIVATING AND EFFECTIVE PERFORMANCE APPRAISAL
- COMMITMENT, MOTIVATION AND TALENT RETENTION
- HOW TO MANAGE RESISTANCE TO CHANGE SUCCESSFULLY
- GENERATIONAL CLASH. MILLENNIALS
- TELEWORK AND VIRTUAL TEAMS

HIGH-PERFORMANCE TEAM

For a company to succeed, it is essential to have a good team, not only competent as individuals, but also able to work well as a team when the occasion demands it. The team leader has a crucial role to play in ensuring that the team achieves high performance.

In my book *Motivated Teams, Productive Teams* I explain the key techniques and methodologies to achieve high performance teams. If you want to go into detail I recommend that you consult it, the feedback from those who have already read it confirms that it is very useful if you are leading a team. In the following pages I will briefly summarize the most relevant points already covered in my previous book and other additional topics, such as talent retention, change management and how to lead millennials.

What is necessary for a team to achieve high performance?

Key 1. Define objectives. The team needs to focus on these common objectives and be very clear about where they need to row. Ideally, the objectives of each individual should be aligned with those of the team. It is important that these objectives are specific, measurable, achievable and relevant. We need to track achievements well.

Key 2. Define the roles of each of the team members, and make sure that this role is in accordance with the profile of each of the individuals. It is important that they complement each other and that the strengths of some compensate for the weaknesses of others.

Key 3. Give clear and constructive feedback, both on what is being done well and what needs to be improved. This is important to keep the team motivated and in line with the expectations we place on them. In this way we will reinforce productive behaviors and will be able to rectify those that are less adequate.

Key 4. Use systems to reward teamwork. When evaluating and rewarding each team member, both individual and team achievements must be assessed.

Key 5. Determine which leadership style is appropriate for each occasion, so that while in some cases a democratic style will be more appropriate, in other cases it may be more appropriate to delegate or, on the contrary, to use a more directive style. The variables to be taken into account to determine the most appropriate style will be: aptitude and attitude of the collaborator, task and situation.

Key 6. Encourage initiative in the team. We will allow our team members to question the way things are done and feel free to contribute new ideas. Encourage constructive criticism and the opportunity to improve existing procedures. It is very important to listen to our team.

Key 7. Identify and retain talent. It is necessary to recruit competent and talented employees, but this is not enough, we must be able to retain that talent so that they can develop their full potential within the team and stay motivated.

Key 8. Error management. It is important for the team to manage mistakes constructively as a way to overcome and move forward. It is important to make the team aware that it is not a matter of looking for guilty parties, but of solving the error, as well as identifying the cause in order to implement preventive measures together.

Key 9. Priority management. To achieve high performance it is essential that the team optimizes the management of their time and priorities, that they are very clear about the difference between urgent and important, prioritizing what is really relevant to achieve their objectives.

Key 10. Continuous training. It is key to invest in the training of the team, so that they have the opportunity to renew their knowledge. This has a double benefit: on the one hand, our employees learn new skills and on the other hand, they are motivated by the fact that the company invests in them.

A team is much more than a group of individuals working together. A good team is interdependent, that is, they have to rely on each other to achieve their objectives.

We will look in more detail at the most significant points in the following chapters.

KEYS TO OPTIMIZE
YOUR LEADERSHIP STYLE

SITUATIONAL LEADERSHIP

When I started leading teams for the first time, I was very fortunate that my company had a *Leadership Development* program, that is, when you lead a team, they sent you to London for two weeks to one of the most prestigious leadership institutes in Europe, to train you in all the tools and skills you might need when it came to leading and managing your team. A great success.

For me this was a before and after. I learned that the way a team is managed can have as much effect on the results as the team itself and that finding the right way to do it can be the key to success.

I learned that there is no single leadership style that is valid for all occasions or for all individuals. The key was to adapt the leadership style to each situation and to each individual, as well as to apply, when the situation demands it, techniques to obtain the greatest potential from the team and from each individual.

One of the most significant lessons learned and that had the greatest impact on the management of my team was Kenneth-Blanchard's concept of Situational Leadership.

The Situational Leadership model is based on the fact that there is no one ideal leadership style for everyone; each style adapts to the different levels of development a team goes through.

And how is this applied?

It is essential to first determine the level of development of the team members in order to choose the appropriate management style.

The initial step is to make a good diagnosis. The steps to follow are:

- Identify the tasks to be performed.
- Evaluate the level of competence of employees to perform these tasks.
- To evaluate the level of motivation and self-confidence of people with respect to the task.

Based on this, we choose the style that best suits the situation:

- **Development level 1: DIRECTING. The leader controls**.
  Employees at this level are relatively new in their position, they are motivated but their competencies are not high in the tasks they have to perform, they lack experience and knowledge. In these cases, the leader controls what to do and how to do it, and has to plan how the necessary skills can be acquired to perform the tasks.

- **Development level 2: COACHING. The leader coaches.**
  The collaborator has low levels of competence and his motivation varies as a consequence of the difficulties, therefore the emotional support of the leader is fundamental. The leader helps them to develop knowledge and skills related to their functions and encourages them to establish relationships of participation and cohesion.

- **Developmental Level 3: SUPPORTING. The leader is supportive.**
  The leader gradually gives up control over decisions, promoting participation and responsibility among team members. The employee has gained more competence and adaptability in various situations, showing good integration, although there may still be a need for increased confidence or motivation.

- **Development level 4: DELEGATING. The leader delegates.**
  The employee has increased his or her performance levels. The experience and confidence elevates their feelings of competence and pride in belonging to the group. The leader stimulates and gives autonomy.

The way a team is managed can have as much effect on results as the team itself.

Based on a good diagnosis, the leader's flexibility is fundamental to apply the different leadership styles according to the situation. At the beginning, when someone is new in his position (as 80% of my team was), the control style is more appropriate to progressively reduce the amount of direction, until the level of involvement of the collaborators in decision

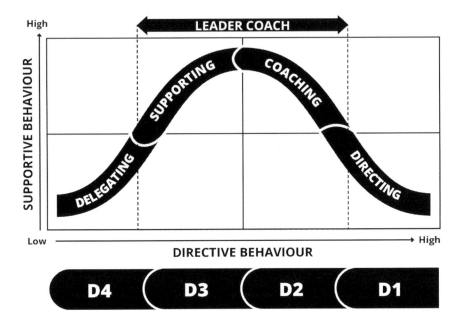

LEADER-COACH

Another of the most useful concepts I learned was how to apply the GROW method with your team members to empower them and help them gain self-confidence while motivating them. When to apply it?

It is true that, although it sounds so good, it requires a significant amount of time and energy. And this is not always available to the team leader.

Therefore, with those individuals who are already motivated and know exactly how to do their job (development level 4), you can simply delegate the task at hand directly (delegation style).

For those who are not experienced or knowledgeable enough (developmental level 1), it may be more appropriate to tell them directly what to do until they become a little more proficient.

That is, if we apply the concept of situational leadership, the leader-coach style would be the appropriate one to apply to individuals at development levels 2 and 3, i.e., those who know how to do the task moderately well or very well but lack sufficient motivation or self-confidence to do it by themselves.

How to apply it?

Here the GROW method fits perfectly and provides us with a structure that facilitates its implementation in a methodical way.

GROW stands for the following words, which coincide with the four steps of the methodology:

- *GOAL:* Objective.
- *REALITY:* Reality.
- *OPTIONS:* Options.
- *WILL:* Action plan.

How could I use this with my team? Well basically everything could be summed up in four questions:

Question 1: What is the problem? With this question the collaborator explains what the objective of the consultation is, or what situation needs to be solved. We are asking him/her to verbalize the problem.

Question 2: How did you try to solve it and what results did you obtain? Here the collaborator explains his/her reality, i.e. everything he/she has tried to solve the problem and how it worked out.

Question 3: And now, what can you do? That is, with this question we are inviting them to generate options. The idea is for them to generate their own alternatives and evaluate their pros and cons.

Question 4: What are you going to do? Once they have generated all these options, we invite them to decide which one seems the most appropriate.

It's amazing how four seemingly simple questions, accompanied by empathy and good active listening, can have such an effect on the motivation and self-confidence of your team members.

This style of leadership, when well applied, helps to motivate and gain the confidence of team members. It's worth a try!

DELEGATE EFFECTIVELY

What is delegation? It is the process of passing on activities, responsibilities and authority to another, while maintaining ultimate responsibility for the outcome. It is not about passing the "hot potato" by relieving yourself of any responsibility (that is not delegating!).

> *Delegating is an excellent opportunity*
> *to motivate,*
> *empower and professionally develop our team.*

These are some of the keys to successful delegation:

Key 1: What to delegate? Not everything can be delegated. It is important that you choose those tasks you are doing that are not directly linked to your goals: small, frequent and repetitive decisions.

Key 2: Who is the most appropriate person to do it? It must be someone who is willing and able to do it. That is, someone who shows the necessary motivation and interest to take on the task and who is also capable of doing it properly. Avoid choosing someone who is already overworked.

Key 3. Meet. It is essential to reach an agreement by letting him/her know that you have total confidence. This step is very important, since we have to involve the person about what is going to be delegated and make sure that he/she agrees to take care of it.

Key 4. Training. This step is fundamental, if the person is not trained to do the task we will hardly have a positive result. We must ensure that we provide the necessary training and information, otherwise we will not only fail to achieve results, but we will frustrate our collaborator.

Key 5. Be accessible for support. It is likely that doubts will arise when performing the task the first few times. Provide the necessary support until your employee feels confident enough to do it independently.

Key 6. Check the key points. If the task to be delegated has some detail of special importance or risk, it is important to highlight it from the beginning. This is key, especially when it comes to preventing problems.

Key 7. Manage their performance. We have to keep track of how it is progressing and if it is doing as expected. If it is not performing, it is a matter of detecting what is going wrong and trying to fix it.

Key 8. Feedback. If something is not being done correctly, it must be indicated from the beginning, in a constructive and clear way. If it is being done correctly, you should also say so.

Key 9. Encourage progress. It is important that we encourage our collaborator to advance in the assigned task, and that he/she perceives it as an opportunity for professional development.

Key 10. Recognition of your achievements. If you have performed the task well.

***Delegating correctly requires time and effort,
but it is an investment that will have a return.***

All this is a brief summary of what I explain, in much more detail, in my book *Motivated Teams, Productive Teams*; in addition, in this book you can consult many other techniques and methodologies to manage people. If you lead a team I recommend you to have it at hand. It will undoubtedly help you in your day-to-day work.

MOTIVATING AND EFFECTIVE
PERFORMANCE APPRAISAL

During the years I worked in Ireland and the Netherlands, every year every employee had a performance review, a meeting with their leader where they were informed of what was expected of them, their objectives, and what they were doing well, poorly, or regularly. For me it was like having a compass that showed me where I had to row.

In the same way, this tool allowed me to transmit and distribute these objectives among the members of my team. That's how we were all rowing in the same direction.

When I returned to Spain, I realized that in our country this tool was hardly used and when it was, it was limited to being a mere formality. It used to be perceived as an "exam" to which the employee was evaluated with a number, a formality of dubious usefulness.

Performance appraisal is one of the most valuable tools a team leader can have. Often it is either not done, or it is not done in a way that the employee perceives as positive and constructive.

However, performance appraisal can be a great opportunity for both the company and the employee. On the one hand, to make clear the objectives that are important for the company and, on the other hand, for the employee to be very clear about what is expected of him, i.e., where he has to put the focus.

The steps for a good performance evaluation are as follows:

STEP 1: OBJECTIVES
Here we will review what is expected of our collaborators. We would review the objectives that were set the previous year and the results achieved; it is important that both parties exchange opinions on what went well, poorly or regularly. We would also have to define objectives for the following year.

STEP 2: ATTITUDES
If in the first part we talked about what to do, here we will review how to do it. We will highlight those attitudes that are most important for each company (they do not have to be the same in all companies). For example, there will be organizations where teamwork is fundamental, others where proactivity or communication or leadership are key.

STEP 3: DEVELOPMENT PLAN
What does our employee need in order to do his or her job better? Where does he or she aspire to go professionally? This third part is perhaps the most motivating for our employee. Here we actively listen to our employee's needs, as well as his or her professional aspirations, and propose an action plan to satisfy them.

A good performance appraisal is a paradigm shift. Instead of asking "what have you done for the organization?", we would ask "what can we do together to achieve better results in the future?".

WHAT ARE THE MOST FREQUENT ERRORS?

These are the most frequent mistakes that I have seen when applying performance evaluation and that make many not have a very positive concept of this methodology.

1- Take it as a mere formality: "In ten minutes we'll do it and that's it".
It is true that a good performance appraisal takes time and can be tedious to prepare if you are not aware of its purpose and benefits. That is why there are organizations that, despite having some kind of evaluation system in place, have not invested time in raising awareness and training, both managers and staff, on the importance of doing it correctly and dedicating time to it. Many managers have deadlines to implement their reviews and when the deadline approaches they do it anyway, thus losing all value.

2- The betting pool: Quick format without giving examples or details.
There are templates that evaluate each objective or quality with a number or with different scales (achieved, partially achieved, not achieved...), and the easiest thing to do is to mark it like a betting pool player. When the interesting and correct thing to do is to give detailed feedback on what has been done well, badly or regularly, with examples and data. Telling someone that his or her objective has been partially achieved is half-heartedly giving feedback. It is necessary to specify in more detail what part has been done well and what has not, with good quality

feedback. This way we give the opportunity to put the focus on where improvement is needed, specifying.

3- The exam: Not listening to their self-evaluation.

Other times it can become a monologue where the person in charge simply gives his opinion on the results and defines the new objectives. The employee may perceive it as an accountability or an examination, when in fact it can be an excellent opportunity to reflect together and make a good self-evaluation on the part of our collaborator. For this to happen, it is necessary to have generated enough trust beforehand. It is as important to evaluate as it is to listen to their self-evaluation, how do they think their performance has been? Where do they think they can improve?

4- Failure to recognize achievements.

If we only focus on the negative part or on what they have not achieved, it is easy for people to feel a certain rejection to this type of procedure. The performance evaluation is an excellent opportunity to provide recognition for a job well done, this will give a motivational boost to our collaborator.

5- Failure to clearly define objectives.

One of the purposes of the performance evaluation should be that our team is very clear about where it has to row, and for this it is essential to define these objectives very clearly, following the SMART model (specific, measurable, achievable, relevant and time-bound).

6- Not preparing the session.

Another very common mistake is not preparing the meeting beforehand, not gathering information, examples, data and the definition of objectives that corresponds to that particular person. This makes the meeting of dubious value. Apart from the fact that we are setting a poor example for our collaborator, if we have not dedicated time to such a crucial meeting, how are we going to inspire our team to stay focused and work in a committed way? How can we demand that they meet objectives that we have not clearly explained and evaluated?

7- Monologue: Do not ask about their needs.
It is important that it does not become a monologue, but that both parties can exchange opinions. Listen to your team's needs, their motivations, their concerns. Simply being listened to already has a motivating effect. Let's ask him and let him express his needs. It is important that he feels listened to and that within the possibilities of the company an action plan is made to cover these needs as much as possible. What does he need to be able to do his job better (training, tools, *software*, etc.)? How would he like to grow professionally?

> *This practice, well implemented, will not only contribute to improve your team's performance, but also to increase their motivation and commitment.*

In conclusion, these are mistakes that should be taken into account when implementing a tool of this type. Maybe you have found some more, are there any other mistakes you would add to this list?

In my book *Motivated Teams, Productive Teams* you have more details on how to implement a good, motivating and effective performance evaluation.

COMMITMENT, MOTIVATION AND TALENT RETENTION

This is an issue that comes up often when I work with my clients in *Leadership Development* processes. They bring up the case of team members who, although they are trained and know their job perfectly well, give them the impression that they don't want to do it.

They are passive or rebellious and do not perform as expected. These cases are often due to problems of motivation or lack of commitment, and can sometimes lead to talent drain.

The difference between "having to do" what needs to be done and "wanting to do it" is marked by the employee's commitment.

BENEFITS OF GENERATING COMMITMENT AND MOTIVATION IN OUR TEAM

Among others, these would be the main benefits of having employees committed to the company:

1. **Higher productivity.** According to a study conducted in the United Kingdom, companies with committed workers can have up to twice as much profit as those that do not.
2. **Improved customer satisfaction.** A committed employee will provide better customer service, which in turn with that positive experience can recommend us and generate more customers.
3. **More stable workforce.** Companies with a high level of commitment have a 40% lower employee turnover rate.
4. **Less absenteeism.** An environment that generates commitment is one where the work climate allows employees to better manage stress, to be absent less often from their work occupation and even the reduction of work-related misfortunes can decrease up to 48% for people who feel satisfied in their companies.
5. **Decrease in conflicts.** An employee who is committed will be less likely to create problems or generate conflicts with both colleagues and managers.

WHAT IS THE IMPACT OF THE TALENT DRAIN?

Losing good employees can have a big impact in many ways:
- Investment of time and money in recruiting new employees.
- Investment of time and money in training and learning curve for new hires.
- Work overload of the rest of the team.
- Negative impact on productivity.
- A rarefied atmosphere in the team.
- Potential impact on end-customer satisfaction.
- Possible domino effect with other workers.

There is no point in recruiting the best employees if they do not remain productive and motivated in our workforces.

Therefore, it is worth the effort to retain talent and prevent it from leaving before it is too late.

WHAT CAN WE DO TO MAINTAIN COMMITMENT AND MOTIVATION?

When we have someone in our team who really contributes, that is, who knows and wants to do their job well, it is something we have to value and take special care of. We should not take it for granted that they will remain like that forever. In addition, they can be a great support for any leader, our right hand in many cases.

> *"There's no point in hiring smart people to tell them what to do; we hire smart people to tell us what to do"* **(Steve Jobs).**

When we recruit talent, it is normal that at the beginning they are motivated and that in a short time they reach a high performance. If we want to keep them that way, we will have to follow the following guidelines:

Participatory definition of objectives. We must adequately define objectives following the SMART format (specific, measurable, achievable, relevant and time-bound). Let's take advantage of our team's talent in the definition of these objectives. When I work with my clients and their teams, the first work sessions are dedicated precisely to this, that is, to define their objectives together and reach a consensus on their definition, how to measure it, whether or not it is achievable and what deadlines to set. This has a great impact on commitment and motivation. Having clearly defined objectives is not exclusive to those with talent, but is crucial for the whole team. Everyone must be clear about what is expected of them and what their contribution is to the company's mission, vision and values.

Co-creation of action plans. Once the objectives have been defined, instead of telling our team what to do, it is much more powerful to co-create the action plan, especially if they are trained professionals with high potential. This can be done both individually and as a team with a good group work session where ideas are generated, evaluated, the best options are selected and finally it is defined what to do, who is going to do it, when and how. It is a good way to take advantage of all that talent.

Autonomy and freedom, which is especially important for high-potential, high-performing employees. Micromanaging or not giving them room for maneuver can ruin the talent of these team members.

Continuous training, so that they can continue to develop their knowledge within the company and can nurture all that potential. It is essential to invest in the training of the team, so that they have the opportunity to renew their knowledge. This has a double benefit: on the one hand, our employees acquire new skills and on the other hand, they generate commitment and motivation when they see that the company invests in them.

Keep your promises, if you offer something that you don't deliver, you will create distrust and disappointments that can undermine the motivation of your team. Sooner or later it will take its toll.

Create a good working environment, where people feel comfortable working, this favors talent retention. There are people who especially value working at ease with their colleagues, especially millennials.

Two-way communication. Communication within a team is fundamental and should never be neglected. Give clear and constructive feedback, both on what is being done well and what needs to be improved. This is important to keep the team motivated and in line with the expectations we place on them. In this way we will reinforce productive behaviors and be able to rectify those that are less adequate, and at the same time ask for feedback on how they feel as part of our team. This will allow us to detect in time and prevent a possible risk of talent drain.

Listen to suggestions and take them into account, this does not mean that all the ideas have to be implemented, but if the team sees that their ideas do not get anywhere, there will come a time when they get frustrated and stop contributing them. Someone who has talent can surely contribute great ideas that will make the company progress.

Healthy and motivating leadership. According to situational leadership theory, there is no one-size-fits-all leadership style; the key is to choose the one that best suits the situation. It is often heard that people don't leave their jobs, they leave their bosses. That is why it is important to invest in leadership skills training for our managers. A *Leadership Development* process can help enormously in these cases.

Professional development. Encourage talent development, not only with training, but also by assigning them new responsibilities and challenges. If they perform well, we could reward them with promotions within the company when possible. There are professionals who leave their company because they have reached a plateau and feel stagnant. That is why it is so important to understand their career aspirations and make a plan that allows them to evolve.

Taking an interest in their needs and building a development plan together certainly gets our people on board.

- **Recognition,** this is perhaps one of the factors that can motivate the most and that does not have to have an economic cost. The great forgotten factor in our companies. It is important that our team feels that their contribution is valued. In addition, surely someone with talent achieves achievements that deserve recognition.

- **Fair salary** in accordance with the value of our collaborator. This point is important, although surprising as it may seem, in some cases it is not the most relevant factor. Especially above certain salaries. I have met many professionals who, once the basic economic needs are covered, give it less importance. There are even workers who, despite having a decent salary, decide to leave for other reasons, since the economic factor does not compensate for other shortcomings they may have in the company.

The ideal is to create an ideal environment where our entire team works at ease, fostering healthy and motivating leadership, clearly defined objectives and making our people feel that their contribution is important to the company.

In conclusion, when we have someone with talent in our team it is important to keep in mind that we must let them grow and develop professionally, offer them challenging goals that will help them to improve themselves and at the same time keep them motivated. As they have a high potential, if they feel that they have stagnated, they could consider looking for growth elsewhere.

Although we must also be careful not to overload too much, sometimes we are not aware that we tend to assign too many tasks to those who are more productive (because they are the ones who "deliver"), and we can reach extremes where that person ends up totally exhausted or stressed by the overload of work.

We have to find the balance between challenging objectives and workload, and how do we do that? Well, with good communication and by observing the warning signs that sometimes speak for themselves.

Motivating a team is not necessarily about a pay raise. Most of the time what really motivates them are: clearly defined objectives, a healthy and motivating leadership, the feeling of being an essential part of the organization and that their work is valued and considered necessary.

WHAT ARE THE WARNING SIGNS?

We must be especially vigilant in these situations:

- Someone who has always performed very well and is now starting to be **less productive.**
- Someone who has always been motivated and suddenly becomes more **apathetic.**

- When signs of **burnout** are evident (we tend to put more work on those who are more productive).
- When someone is highly **stressed**, they may decide to choose their health over work.
- When someone **stops contributing ideas** and suggestions, whereas they used to, it is a clear symptom that they have lost the interest they once had.

If we detect this risk of leakage and do nothing, we will most likely end up losing this valuable member of our team and we will have to assume the consequences. It is essential that we take care of our employees.

IS IT AN ISOLATED OR RECURRENT CASE?

It is worth noting whether we have had an isolated case of lack of motivation or talent drain, or whether it is something that is repeated over time. If it is something recurrent, it is worth analyzing what may be going wrong in our team and taking the necessary measures to solve it; it may be helpful to turn to professionals for advice. It is often difficult to get an objective view of what is really going on from the inside. When someone who is an expert in the field and neutral analyzes the situation can give us a diagnosis of what is happening and the keys to solve it.

WHAT CAN WE DO TO RETAIN TALENT?

It is important to be alert and pick up on these signals to act as soon as possible, otherwise it may be too late.

Apart from all of the above, there are additional actions that would be key:

Apply leader-coach methodologies: In case of lack of commitment or motivation in our team, the most appropriate leadership style is democratic or participative, in other words, the one that establishes a two-way communication between leader and collaborator.

Quality communication: In these cases it is crucial that we communicate with them, that we show our concern and our intention to improve the situation.

Listening: It is essential that we listen very carefully, sometimes common sense and a good observation can be our best allies. Listen to their suggestions, motivations and needs.

Find out what they need: Both by asking and listening to our collaborator directly, as well as from other sources (maybe he has commented something to a colleague or we can review old emails that we never answered). Who knows, there is a lot of information that we sometimes overlook and that can give us the keys to what is going on.

Action plan: Take action and make sure you do what you can to meet their needs (as long as they are reasonable), sometimes it is not possible to grant everything they ask for, but simply knowing that you are listening and that you intend to do something about it can help a lot.

These guidelines, when properly applied, can help you regain motivation and commitment in your team and retain talent. It's worth a try!

And finally, I would like to recall an excerpt from Daniel Goleman, author of *Emotional Intelligence in Business*:

> *"Those who value the company's purpose and embrace it are not only willing to go the extra mile for it, but also to make personal sacrifices when necessary. They are the ones who will work late into the night or over a weekend to get a project done on time; they are the managers who are willing to leave on a moment's notice when an urgent matter arises".*

HOW TO MANAGE RESISTANCE
TO CHANGE SUCCESSFULLY

Are you implementing changes in your company and your team is resisting? Would you like to know what to do to get your people on board with the change? Lately several of my clients are experiencing situations like this in their teams. They find themselves with the need to implement changes, but they see that their teams don't make it easy for them.

Our society is constantly changing, and it is essential that companies and their teams know how to adapt to these changes if they want to survive. However, change is difficult, especially in organizations.

Some time ago I heard a quote from Darwin that said:

"It is neither the strongest nor the smartest that survives, but the one that best adapts to change."

In recent months, consultants specializing in digitization of companies, or even engineering companies specializing in cutting-edge technology, have asked me to collaborate because they are realizing that in many of the projects they carry out with their clients, the biggest difficulty they are encountering has nothing to do with the technological part, but with the resistance of the people who have to change the way they work. That is why they seek my collaboration, to overcome that tremendous barrier, which is resistance to change, and that can ruin the most innovative of projects.

According to a post by *Meliorate* the causes why change implementation can fail within organizations are as follows:

- 39% employee resistance to change.
- 33% the behavior of the management team.
- 14% lack of resources.
- 14% other obstacles.

As we can see from these statistics, the human factor accounts for no less than 72% of the total causes of failure.

WHY DO THEY RESIST CHANGE?

These may be the main reasons why our employees may resist change:

1- **The unknown generates insecurity**, the old saying "better the known bad than the unknown good" resonates in many organizations.
2- **Not feeling the need to change,** when you think that the way you are doing things is working well.
3- When the **reason for the change** is unclear or not understood.
4- When they do **not feel capable of** assuming these changes.

5- When it involves changing **habits and routines.**

6- **Lack of confidence** that these changes can be successfully managed.

7- When they **have not been involved in** decision making or have not been asked for their opinion.

8- **Lack of** adequate **information** and communication.

9- **Lack of motivation.**

10- **Fear** of how these changes will affect their work (more workload or the opposite, that the position is no longer necessary).

WHAT CAN WE DO?

Here are some keys to overcome these resistances within our teams.

Key 1: What are the risks of staying as we are? When insecurity in the face of the unknown arises, we should ask ourselves: What security will we have if we do not change? Are the risks or "dangers" of not changing greater than those of staying as we are?

Key 2: Benefits. Be clear about the benefits: What will it mean for the company? And for its customers? And for its employees?

Key 3: Training. It is important that they do not feel lost and that they can acquire the necessary skills and abilities, especially when it comes to technological changes.

Key 4: Create new habits and routines. It will probably be necessary to unlearn in order to relearn. To do this it is important to keep in mind that it takes at least twenty-one days to build new habits, and it is better to go slowly, especially with those who are more reluctant to change.

Key 5: Small steps. The Kaizen philosophy tells us that small changes can lead to big transformations. What is the smallest change that can be implemented in the desired direction? When that small change has been implemented, you can start with the next one.

Key 6: Involve our teams in the processes. Involving our team in the change will not only reduce the risk of resistance, but they will also be able to provide us with very interesting information (new ideas, needs, possible unforeseen events, etc.). It is important to agree on goals with our teams in terms of the changes to be implemented, dates, etc.

Key 7: Clear communication at all levels. We must resolve any doubts about what changes are going to be made, what for, when, how, who, where, etc. Lack of communication generates confusion and false rumors, and this generates resistance.

Key 8: Reward. It would be convenient if the team could have some kind of award or recognition in the short term to motivate them to keep moving forward in the process of change. It is also important to celebrate each achievement.

Key 9: Generate confidence in the process. Encourage them to express their doubts and concerns, which we must try to resolve in a way that makes them feel an important part of the change.

Key 10: Adaptability. We must take into account each individual, each organization and type of change we are implementing. A change related to digital transformation is not the same as a change related to the reorganization of a company's organization chart, we have to find the formula that best suits each case.

It is clear that in our times the only sure thing is change, and the better we prepare our teams for it, the more likely we are to succeed in adapting to it.

GENERATIONAL CLASH: MILLENNIALS

A few months ago a CEO told me: "Inma, I don't know what to do anymore, new hires are leaving me one after the other a few months after starting". This CEO was desperate, specifically, he had a position that had been without anyone stable for two years because none of the candidates who were selected and hired stayed.

After analyzing the situation my conclusion was clear, the problem was the generational clash, the leadership style that had given this CEO such good results for years, and that continued to give good results with the older members of his team, had stopped working with the new generations: Millennials.

Millennials are considered to be those born between 1980 and 2000, and it is estimated that in 2025 they will make up no less than 75% of the working population.

To put us in the picture, let's take a look at the different generations:

- **Baby boomers:** Born from 1946 to 1964. This group values work, perseverance, honesty and loyalty. They consider that their company is the only one of their entire career because in their scale the weight tends to the security and stability it provides.

- **Generation X:** Born between 1965 and 1980. They have adapted to the advent of the Internet and like to work in teams. They have aspirations and desire professional development within the same company, and are willing to demand from the company what they believe is necessary to meet their expectations of personal satisfaction.

- **Millennials:** Born between 1980 and 2000. This generation is driven by a job that makes them happy. They are not afraid of change and are always willing to undertake. A very remarkable characteristic of millennials is that they adapt easily to a changing pace in projects and assume failure as part of success.

- **Generation Z:** These are people born after 2000. Many of them are studying or starting to set foot in the working world. They manage technology and social networks very well and are characterized by being self-taught thanks to the information provided by the Internet.

Each generation will have a leadership style that works better than another, and they will have different motivators. For example, a baby boomer may be motivated by financial rewards. While for generation X, development and growth programs within the company would be effective.

What works with millennials? What does a leader who begins to incorporate members of the new generations into his or her team have to take into account?

Here are some guidelines that can help you adapt your leadership style to millennials, since this is a group that is growing in companies. If you are also a millennial you will have it easier because you will share the same mentality, but if you are not, here are some tips that will help you:

1- Leadership style. If a millennial is not comfortable with the leadership style in their company, they will not hesitate to leave. They are looking for less pyramidal and more participative leadership structures. Rigid, authoritarian and autocratic structures do not work with these generations. They need leaders who are democratic, participative, inspirational and who lead by example.

2- Participation. They need their opinion to be heard, to be given and asked for feedback in a constructive way. It is important to ensure that communication flows and that they can contribute their ideas, that we can involve them in decisions, projects and what is expected of them. To reach a consensus on objectives and make them co-creators of the action plans to achieve those objectives.

3- Balance between professional and personal life. They do not live to work, they work to live. They value working for results more than working marathon days. Flexibility to choose the place and time to work, more and more, and thanks to new technologies this is becoming easier. Flexibility of schedules is increasingly valued among the new generations.

4- Development. Providing the necessary training and education to enable them to take on new challenges. Technical advances are becoming faster and faster and they value the support they need to tackle them successfully. Generating opportunities for growth and development. Being generations that have grown up in the culture of immediacy and surrounded by stimuli (especially those born in the nineties), they are impatient and eager for new experiences, and are especially stimulated by short-term challenges with visible results. That's why their leaders must help them identify opportunities to develop their skills and see that they are evolving.

5- The relative value of money. Money is not everything, as long as basic needs are covered, of course. Unlike other generations where the economic reward had a great motivating effect, in these generations not everything is paid for by money and it is not the most important thing. They may value more having more time, more flexibility, a job in line with their values, or where they can contribute their ideas...

6- The values and culture of the company. Millennials feel the need to work for structures and organizations that are aligned with what they consider ethical and important.

7- Recognition. If this is already important for the vast majority of people, for millennials it is even more so. Moreover, this is one of the pending issues of most companies and on the other hand is one of the gestures that most boosts the motivation of any worker.

Many may think that millennials are the ones who have to adapt to their traditional leadership styles, since that is what has always worked. However, it is a fact that the new generations are here to stay, and little by little they will become a majority that will set new leadership trends in our companies. Undoubtedly, those companies that are able to adapt their leadership style to this generational change will be the ones that achieve the best results.

This is why there is a need to train their managers, all those leading teams, in more effective forms of leadership with the new generations.

If you are a millennial and your boss is not, I hope you are now clearer about how each generation has a different mentality, and I invite you to review the chapter where I talk about the keys to manage your boss, sure it will help you to smooth the differences.

TELEWORK AND VIRTUAL TEAMS

My first experience with teleworking was when I lived in the Netherlands more than a decade ago. I had to drive 45 kilometers round trip every day, and my pregnancy made me drowsy. One day while driving I almost had an accident. I talked to my boss, and we agreed to work one day a week at the office and the rest from home. The experience was new to me and was positive for both parties.

At this moment, as I am writing the last pages of this book, we are confined due to the pandemic of the Covid-19 virus. An unprecedented situation that has forced us to telework. Some of us have been doing it for years, but for others it is something new.

For managers, the challenge is not only to telework, but also to manage their teams remotely.

There are companies that already practiced remote work in whole or in part, but for others it was not only something new, but they were not yet ready to take this step.

If managing teams is already complex in itself, doing it remotely is a challenge, especially if it has not been done before.

We will now review some guidelines that can help us when managing teams remotely.

Clearly defined objectives
When teleworking, we usually do not have to stick to a fixed working schedule (except for some specific cases, such as customer service positions, etc.). Therefore, to manage a team that we cannot see, we have to be results-based. In other words, set clearly defined objectives and let them choose how to organize themselves. The important thing is that the work is done correctly and on time.

As leaders, it is our responsibility to clearly define tasks and goals for each member of our team. When we do so, we will avoid misunderstandings and ambiguities if we follow the SMART (specific, measurable, achievable, relevant and time-bound) format explained earlier in this book.

Managing performance
If managing performance and giving feedback is crucial in on-site teams, it is even more important in remote teams. The team leader must be able to monitor whether or not the team is achieving the objectives set. Therefore, we will establish ways to measure progress and give feedback *to* guide them appropriately. The way to do this will depend on the activity, type of company and preferences of each team. KPIs can be established, reports with a certain frequency (daily, weekly, etc.) or perhaps video calls. To achieve better results and greater commitment, it is advisable to agree with the team both the parameters and the way to do this monitoring.

Generate an environment of trust and commitment
Undoubtedly, when we have a team teleworking it is important to have previously built a culture of trust, commitment and

self-responsibility. This is usually not done overnight, and will depend largely on the leader. It is so crucial that we have dedicated a whole chapter to this topic.

Healthy and motivating leadership

We have already seen that practicing a healthy and motivating leadership style is key to developing a high performance team. Having a leader who empowers the team and leads by example is one of the key ingredients for a team to achieve good results while telecommuting. Working remotely can be hard for some team members, the leader must be able to adapt his leadership style to provide each of its members what is required at all times, some will need more direction, others more autonomy. We must be attentive to the needs of each one, and when in doubt, ask them how we can help them.

Communication

Information flow is crucial for a team to function, especially when team members are not in the same location. When working remotely, the physical and visual contact of the workspace is lost and it is important to implement processes and tools to ensure that everyone receives information properly.

For this purpose, it would be convenient to establish certain rules with the team, ideally agreeing on the following points:

- Preferred means of communication: e-mail, telephone, video call, WhatsApp...
- How to communicate emergencies.
- Videoconference meetings (platform, frequency, participants...).
- Use of chat rooms for spontaneous communications.
- Project follow-up.
- Conflict management.

Effective videoconferencing

As we have seen, communication in remote teams is essential, since distance can complicate the way we work. For this, videoconferencing can be a good ally, especially because we can read non-verbal language, which accounts for more than 90% of the message we transmit when communicating.

For a videoconference to be really effective, it is important to follow certain guidelines, such as those we saw earlier in this book, although with certain nuances:

-Plan it in advance: objective, date and time, duration, topics to be discussed, participants...
-Doing your "homework," i.e., making sure that you prepare in advance the information you need to review, discuss or share.
-Ensure an adequate connection: that everyone has access to the platform (Skype, Zoom or similar), good connection, webcam, audio, etc., and also knows how it works.
-Send connection link if necessary, well in advance and connect a few minutes before to avoid last minute problems.
-Preparing a good presentation that can be shared can be a great help when explaining complex topics.
-Make brief written minutes summarizing the session: attendees, discussion, action plan, date of next meeting....

Collaborative work tools

In remote teams, and especially when there are tasks where several team members are involved, it is important to rely on tools that facilitate collaborative work. Some of these tools are particularly useful:

-Platforms for virtual meetings: Skype, Zoom, etc.
-Tools for project management: Trello, Slack...

-File sharing spaces: Dropbox, Google Drive...
-Sending of large files: WeTransfer...

Training

Teleworking can be something totally new for some employees, and a big change in the way they do their daily tasks and communicate. In some cases, the use of new tools can overwhelm our employees. To avoid resistance to these changes and to make it easier for work and communication to flow, it is important to provide training and coaching in the use of the new technologies being used. This training should be adapted to the needs of each individual.

In the case of teams that already have some of their members with experience and knowledge in these tools, they can act as mentors or tutors for their colleagues. In this way, training is streamlined and teamwork is encouraged.

Managing cultural diversity

Sometimes you work remotely with professionals from other countries. I have experienced firsthand what cultural diversity means: I worked for ten years outside Spain and in the first team I led we had seven different nationalities. It is essential to keep in mind that these cultural differences can otherwise be a source of conflict. It is key to keep an open mind, in the face of any misunderstanding.

My first team was based in the Netherlands, but we spoke English among ourselves which, for most, was not our native language. In this scenario it is not uncommon to have misunderstandings due to language. This becomes even more complicated when communication is at a distance. It is therefore advisable to summarize in writing the main issues agreed upon after a call.

You also have to take into account time differences, customs, gestures, etc. I talk about all this in one of my lectures that you can find on my Youtube channel.

To sum up, in case of multicultural teams, it is highly recommended to be informed about the possible cultural differences of our employees and to cultivate an open mind within the team.

Conclusion
In conclusion, teleworking is something that is on the rise and it is essential that both we and our teams are prepared to adapt to this way of working. Let's get ready for it and optimize the way we work remotely.

EPILOGUE

If you have made it to the end of this book, I hope it has provided value to you.

And I also hope that it hasn't just meant a few hours of reading for you. My goal with this book is to help you make your day-to-day life easier, more productive and satisfying. So don't put this book in a drawer or on a shelf and forget about it.

It's not what you learn,
is what you do with what you learn.

I would like you to make a small reflection on what you can change in your daily life, what you can apply from what you have read here, and with it make an action plan specifying what you are going to do, when you are going to implement it, how you are going to implement it, with whom you are going to practice it, where you are going to apply it.

I encourage you to put it in writing and follow up weekly, or at least monthly.

We can learn many leadership theories from the best professors, researchers, consultants, but a true leader is forged when he or she puts all this knowledge into practice in real situations and with real teams.

What you really learn
is internalized and makes a difference,
is what is practiced.

No one can be an expert in team leadership if they haven't experienced it firsthand. That's when you can really see what works and what doesn't in the real world. That's why I encourage you to put what you've learned into action from day one. Adapt it to your particular situation, your team, your industry and your company. Make it your own and make the most of it.

Thank you very much for reading this book.

DO YOU WANT TO FURTHER DEVELOP YOUR LEADERSHIP?

If this is your case, I recommend that you visit my website www.inmarios.com, where you can consult all the resources I make available to managers and their teams.

-Leadership Development Programs.
-In Company Training.
-Online training.
-Books.
-Conferences.

Also, I would like to invite you to follow my social networks, especially LinkedIn. Also, if you subscribe to my newsletter, I will keep you up to date with my latest posts on leadership and team management and all the events related to the topic in which I participate.

ABOUT INMA RÍOS

Inma Ríos is an expert in Leadership Development and High Performance Teams, an engineer from the Polytechnic University of Valencia. International speaker. Author of the leadership books *Motivated Teams, Productive Teams* and *Keys to Lead Successfully*. Top Women Leaders 2022 Award.

She has managed Supply Chain departments at EMEA level (Europe, Middle East and Africa), managing suppliers, production and multidisciplinary and multicultural teams.
She has **20 years of professional experience in multinationals in various European countries** (Ireland, the Netherlands and France), and although he returned to Spain in 2007, she continued working for other international environments.

Inma has first-hand experience of leading teams in complex and challenging environments. She knows how it feels to be under pressure and how to stay motivated, as well as how to achieve positive results in difficult situations. That is why his approach is based on **practical and effective solutions** that can be implemented in any team's day-to-day work.

Since 2013 he has been a consultant and trainer for organisations and business schools. He has helped more than 100 companies to develop high-performance teams and has trained thousands of managers to develop the mindset and skills of great leaders in order to achieve more motivated and productive teams. He has more than 5000 students from all over the world in his *online* video courses. His podcast *Train Your Leadership!* is listened to in more than 30 countries.

Her most relevant qualifications include: Professor of several MBA programmes at FBS Fundesem Business School, teacher and consultant accredited by the School of Industrial Organisation. Master's Degree in *Coaching* with NLP and Emotional Intelligence accredited by ICF (International Coach Federation). Professional Coach certified by ASESCO (Spanish *Coaching Association*), Systemic Team *Coaching* by the Academy of Executive Coaching in London. Certified Behavioural and Motivational Analyst by TTI Talent Insights. Scrum Master. Certified Agile Team Facilitator by IC Agile (ICP- ATF) in the UK.

You can access their website, social networks, books, videocourses, etc. in this QR.

OTHER BOOKS BY INMA RÍOS

KEYS TO SUCCESSFUL LEADERSHIP
Developing the Mindset and Skills of a Great Leader

Have you just been promoted to a position of greater responsibility? Do you aspire to become a great leader?

The purpose of this book is to provide these professionals who suddenly find themselves in a new situation (a team in charge, increased responsibilities, new roles, etc.) with a guide to help them achieve better results.

Also available in Spanish.

PRODUCTIVITY FOR LEADERS
A Practical Guide to Time Management
and Stress Reduction

Feeling overwhelmed?
"Productivity for Leaders" offers a roadmap to success.
This guide tackles time management, stress reduction, and
techniques to empower you and your team.
Learn to prioritize, manage interruptions, and optimize
meetings. Discover strategies for remote teams and personal
well-being, to achieve peak productivity in today's
demanding business world.

Also available in Spanish.

MOTIVATED TEAMS, PRODUCTIVE TEAMS:
A Practical Guide for Leaders

Struggling to lead a high-performing team?
"Motivated Teams, Productive Teams" offers practical guidance for managers and supervisors. Explore the secrets to boosting team motivation and productivity.
Discover how to create a motivating work environment, set clear goals, and implement effective communication strategies. Learnto recognize and reward contributions.
Invest in your team's success .

Also available in Spanish.

MORE RESOURCES

AND SOCIAL NETWORKS

If you liked this book and are interested in following my contents in the future, here are some options:

Newsletter on LinkedIn: Where I publish a weekly article that will be sent to you as soon as you subscribe.

I invite you to visit **my website www.inmarios.com** and to subscribe to my mailing list. You will receive first-hand information about new books, courses, special promotions and other interesting topics.

Listen to my **podcast _¡ENTRENA TU LIDERAZGO!_ (only available in Spanish)** where you can listen to my content while driving, exercising or doing other things. You can find it on various platforms: Spotify, Google Podcasts, Apple Podcast, Anchor, Ivoox, Breaker, Pocket Cast, Radio Public...

Social media. I invite you to share your inspiration by posting that phrase or whatever has caught your attention from this book on social networks and to tag me so that it reaches me, so I can greet you with a message.

LinkedIn (www.linkedin.com/in/inmarios/)
Instagram (@inmarios_)
Twitter (@inmarios_)
YouTube (www.youtube.com/c/INMARIOS)
Facebook (@InmaRiosFB)

You can access my website, social networks, my books, video courses, etc. in this QR.

PROFESSIONAL SERVICES

OF INMA RÍOS

I work mainly **in-company** with **management teams and middle management** to develop healthy and motivating leadership by training them in practical tools that help tremendously in the management of their teams. This is possible both in group and individual format.

I also guide companies and their leaders in the **Development of High Performance Teams,** making a diagnosis of their teams in order to get to know them better and identify strengths and areas for improvement. In my workshops, everyone participates actively and dynamically, leading to greater commitment and motivation, thus improving results.

To this end, I combine three disciplines: training, *mentoring* and de- The following options are available for personal development:

LEADERSHIP DEVELOPMENT: For managers and middle managers who wish to develop healthy and motivating leadership, training them in practical tools that help tremendously in the management of their teams. Group or individual modality can be chosen.

DEVELOPING HIGH-PERFORMANCE TEAMS:
By diagnosing your teams in order to get to know them better and to identify strengths and areas for improvement. Advice is given on the definition of objectives and the co-creation of action plans together with their collaborators. This takes place in workshops where everyone participates actively and dynamically, leading to a greater commitment to achieving these goals and, therefore, greatly improving results and motivation.

IN COMPANY TRAINING: Can be chosen from a menu of workshops or customised according to the needs of each team: leadership, time management, assertive communication, etc.

ONLINE TRAINING: Can be chosen from the menu of workshops or customised according to the needs of each team: leadership, time management, assertive communication, etc.

LECTURES: Dynamic, agile presentations with valuable content, including anecdotes and personal experiences to inspire with freshness in company events and other organisations.

Do you need more information? I invite you to visit my website
www.inmarios.com

BIBLIOGRAPHY

- 50Minutos.es. (2016). El principio de Pareto: Optimice su negocio con la regla del 80/20. España: 50Minutos.es.
- Allen. D. (2015).Getting Things Done: The Art of Stress-free Producti- vity. (English Edition). Londres: Reino Unido: Piatkus.
- Altman, H. (2017). KANBAN: Guía Ágil Paso a Paso Diseñada Para Ayudar a los Equipos a Trabajar Juntos de Manera Más Eficiente (Kanban in Spanish/ Kanban en Español).
- Alonso Puig, M. (2010). Reinventarse. (Plataforma Actual). (20ª ed.). Barcelona, España: Plataforma Editorial.
- Belbin. (2008). La guía Belbin para triunfar en el trabajo. Bilbao, España: Belbin Associates.
- Blanchard, K., Zirgami, P., & Zirgami, D. (2000). Leadership and the One Minute Manager. Nueva York, Estados Unidos: HarperCollins.
- Bolton, R. (2009). People Styles at Work... And Beyond. (2ª ed.). Nashville, Estados Unidos: AMACOM.
- Blatto, L. E. (2012, 16 enero). «6 consejos para reconocer la la- bor del trabajador».
- Covey, S. R. (1989). The 7 Habits of Highly Effective People. (Ed. rev.). Londres, Reino Unido: DK.
- Covey, S. R. (2013). El octavo hábito. Barcelona, España: Paidós Ibérica.
- Diario de Navarra (edición digital). (2016, 15 noviembre). «Una empresa con trabajadores felices puede aumentar su

productividad hasta un 31%».

- Expansión. (2019, 3 julio). «Estar quemado ya es una enferme- dad oficialmente».
- Fastcompany. (2014, 4 julio). «5 Ways To Save Your Middle Mana- ger From Burnout».
- Fundació Factor Humá. (2016, mayo). «Herramientas de auto- conocimiento en el ámbito laboral».
- Galindo, L. (2014). Reilusionarse. (10ª ed.). Barcelona, España: Alienta.
- Gebelein, S. H., Nelson-Neuhaus, C. J., Skube, C. J., Stevens, L. A., Hellervick, L. W., & Davis, B. L. (2010). Successful Manager's Hand- book. (8ª ed.). Roswell, Estados Unidos: PreVisor, Inc.
- Goleman, D (1996). Inteligencia emocional. Barcelona, España: Editorial Kairós.
- Goleman, D. (2018).Inteligencia emocional en la empresa (Im- prescindibles). Barcelona, España: Conecta.
- Goleman, D. (2006). Inteligencia social. Barcelona, España: Editorial Planeta.
- Goleman, D. (2014). Liderazgo. El poder de la inteligencia emocional. Barcelona, España: B DE BOOKS.
- Harvard Business Review. (2015). Performance Reviews. Cambridge, Estados Unidos: Harvard University.
- Hawkings, P. (2011). Leadership Team Coaching: Developing Collective Transformational Leadership. Londres, Reino Unido: Kogan Page.
- Heller, R. (1997). How to Delegate. (Essential Managers Series). Westham, Reino Unido: DK.
- Lasa Gómez, C., Álvarez García, A. y De las Heras del Dedo, R. (2017). Métodos Ágiles. Scrum, Kanban, Lean. (Manuales Imprescindibles). Madrid, España: Anaya.
- Lombardo, M. M., & Eichinger, R. W. (2004). FYI: For Your Improvement, A Guide for Development and Coaching (4ª

ed.). Minneapolis, Estados Unidos: Lominger Ltd Inc. 162.

- López, A. (2017). Cliente digital, vendedor digital: Conoce las claves del social selling. (EMPRESA). Barcelona, España: Códice.
- Martel, A. (2014). Gestión práctica de proyectos con Scrum: Desarrollo de software ágil para el Scrum Master. (Aprender a ser mejor gestor de proyectos nº 1). España: Antonio Martel.
- Maurer, R. y Fiszbein, M. R. (2015). Un pequeño paso puede cambiar tu vida: El método Kaizén. Barcelona, España: Ediciones Urano.
- Nir, M., & Berniz, A. (2014). Coaching y liderazgo: Liderando equipos altamente efectivos Guía práctica de coaching de equipos de alto rendimiento. Estados Unidos, Estados Unidos: Generalmanagers.Org.
- Retos Directivos. (2017, 31 marzo). «¿Empresas felices = empresas productivas?». Recuperado 2 diciembre, 2017, de https://retos-directivos.eae.es/empresas-felices-empresasproductivas
- Ríos, I. (2018). Equipos motivados, equipos productivos. Madrid, España: Ed. Tébar Flores.
- Romero Martín, J. M. y Romero Nieva, J. (2019). Lidera tu empresa en la cuarta revolución. Antequera, Málaga, España: ExLibric Antequera, Málaga, España: ExLibric.
- Spencer, S. M., & Spencer, L. M. (1993). Competence at Work: A Model for Superior Performance. Hoboken, Nueva Jersey, Estados Unidos: John Wiley & Sons.
- The Muse. «How to Deal With Burnout as a Manager». Recuperado de: https://www.themuse.com/advice/how-to-deal-withburnout-as-a-manager
- Thornton, C. (2016). Group and Team Coaching: The secret life of groups. Abingdon, Reino Unido: Taylor & Francis.
- Thrive Global. (2019, 26 julio). «New Research Shows

Managers are at an Increased Risk of Stress and Burnout – Her's How to Fight Back». Recuperado de https://thriveglobal.com/stories/managers-management-challenges-avoid-stress-burnout/

- Whitmore, J. (2018). Coaching: El método para mejorar el rendimiento de las personas. (Empresa). Barcelona, España: Ediciones Paidós.
- Wolfe, I. (2004). Understanding Business Values and Motivators. Atlanta, Estados Unidos: Creative Communication Publications.

WEBGRAPHY

- https://www.aden.org/business-magazine/inteligencia-emocional-empresa/
- https://www.businessballs.com/self-management/paretos-80-20-rule-theory/
- https://inmarios.com/blog/
- https://www.inspiringleadershipnow.com/how-to-use-the-pareto-principle-80-20-rule/
- https://jordisanchez.info/que-es-gtd/
- https://luisolavea.xyz/que-es-gtd/
- http://www.mytimemanagement.com/pareto-principle.html
- https://www.psicoactiva.com/blog/la-inteligencia-social-en-que-consiste/
- https://sebastianpendino.com/aumentar-productividad-gtd-principios/
- https://sebastianpendino.com/gtd-getting-things-done/
- https://superrhheroes.sesametime.com/que-es-el-metodo-gtd/

.

Made in the USA
Columbia, SC
02 December 2024

3cafdc24-21b8-4464-8e41-b1e412b28333R01